CLUB ROUTE IN EUROPE

FIELD MARSHAL VISCOUNT MONTGOMERY OF ALAMEIN GCB, DSO,
WITH
LIEUTENANT-GENERAL SIR BRIAN G. HORROCKS, KBE, CB, DSO, MC

CLUB ROUTE IN EUROPE

The Story
of 30 Corps in the European Campaign

compiled by

Ronald Gill and John Groves

The Naval & Military Press Ltd

Published by

The Naval & Military Press Ltd
Unit 10 Ridgewood Industrial Park,
Uckfield, East Sussex,
TN22 5QE England

Tel: +44 (0) 1825 749494
Fax: +44 (0) 1825 765701

www.naval-military-press.com
www.military-genealogy.com

CONTENTS

LIST OF MAPS

Erratum — on the map facing page 68 — the 82nd US Airborne Division is wrongly described as 84th US Airborne Division.

LIST OF ILLUSTRATIONS

PREFACE

That simple sign, the Ace of Clubs, is well known to the hundreds of thousands of fighting men of 30 Corps who journeyed up "Club Route" on their way to victory during the recent war.

Since 1941, 30 Corps had fought its way across the deserts of Africa to Tunis, where the enemy was finally defeated. Then Sicily was invaded, and, after victory there, the Corps returned to England to prepare for the final blow.

With a footing gained on the Continent, the famous Club Route was opened. Through Normandy and Picardy, through Belgium and Holland, in the Ardennes and in the Rhineland, over the Rhine and the Ems and the Weser, to final victory near Bremen, the long road marked by that famous Ace of Clubs went on.

Well known, too, is the Corps sign, a Wild Boar rampant on a white field, affectionately known as "The Old Pig". It is to recall the progress of The Old Pig along Club Route on the Continent that this book has been compiled. It consists of a simple history of the Corps' many battles, together with personal stories of adventure of the fighting troops, contributed by the men themselves.

Many men with a good story to tell had already left 30 Corps by the time this book was begun, and, as a consequence, innumerable brave tales remain untold. Some will feel that they have been left out in the cold, and this is regretted.

But if all the stories of all the fighting men of 30 Corps were to be recorded, then a whole library of books would be needed. The compilers hope that this one volume will provide pleasant reading for an idle hour, and bring back memories of Club Route and The Rampant Boar.

Nienburg
December 1945

Ronald Gill
John Groves

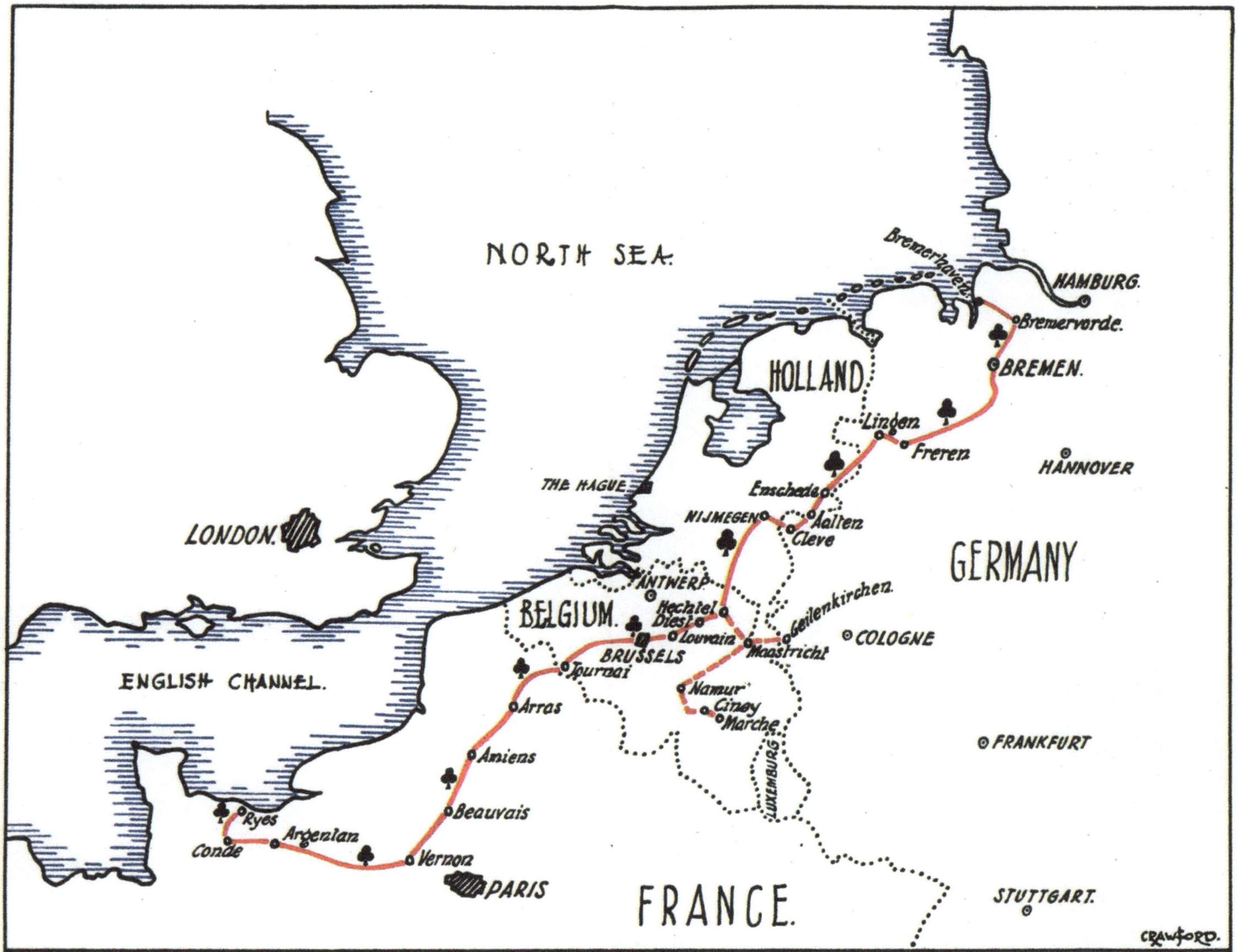

♣ CLUB ROUTE. ♣

Miles 100 50 0 100 200 Miles.

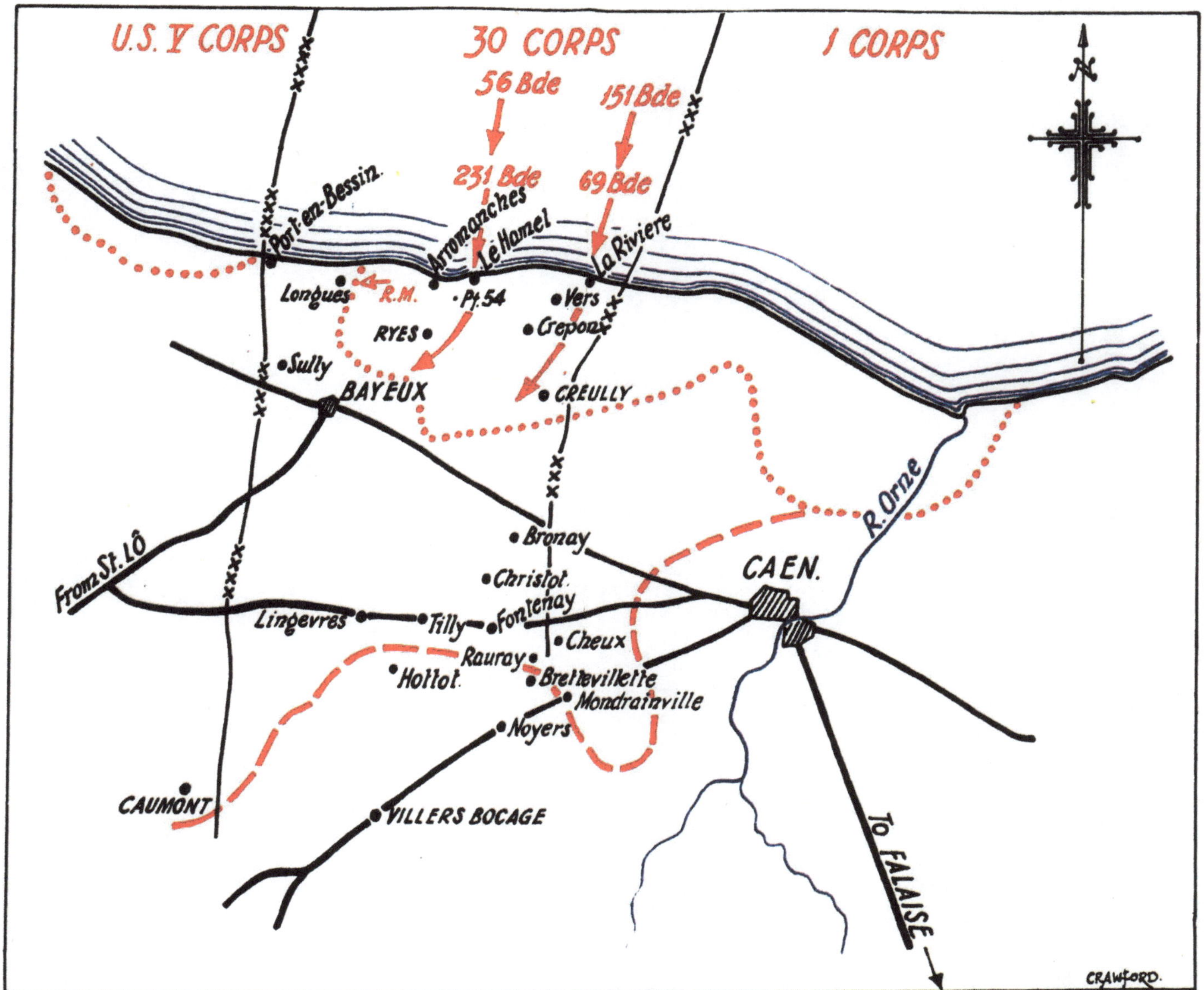

CLUB ROUTE BEGINS.

LINE GAINED AT MIDNIGHT 6 JUNE. ••••••

LINE GAINED AT MIDNIGHT 30 JUNE. — — —

SCALE : 1 : 300,000.

0 5 10

• Miles •

CHAPTER ONE

CLUB ROUTE BEGINS

Since William of Normandy landed near Pevensey and destroyed the English army at Hastings in the year 1066, no would-be invader has ever succeeded in transporting his armies across that narrow obstacle, the English Channel. Philip of Spain tried with his Armada, and there was Napoleon with his "flat bottoms". In 1940 Hitler, with his fleets of barges, and his airforces all ready, was prevented from making the attempt only by the magnificent performance of the RAF, which successfully stopped what was, in fact, the first wave of the invasion.

The British, it has been said, know never when they are beaten. Perhaps that had never before been so true than at the period shortly after our departure from Dunkirk. Driven out of France and Belgium without an ally, seemingly without a hope, we had the audacity to begin making our plans for a return to the Continent. We planned on a vast scale an assault on an enemy who had overrun Europe and looked very much like conquering the world.

As the years passed, and our endless defeats were turned to endless victories, as Egypt, Libya and Sicily were cleared of the enemy, those plans began to take shape, until it became clear at last in 1944 that the Allied invasion must soon break over the shores of Hitler's Fortress Europe.

Training of all branches of the forces for this gigantic task had been long and intensive. Dotted around the coasts of England, Scotland and Wales, were special training areas, and in places civilians had been completely evacuated for security reasons.

Preparations had gone forward steadily, and by June 1st all arrangements had been completed, and the troops and armour were ready in their concentration areas.

Soon after its return from Sicily it became known that 30 Corps was to play a major part in the forthcoming assault on the

German West Wall. The 21st Army Group, commanded by General Sir Bernard Montgomery, consisted of the First US Army, the Second British Army and the First Canadian Army. These armies were to be supported by a large Allied Naval Expeditionary Force, and 6,000 aircraft of the Allied Air Forces.

Operation "Overlord" was the code name for the assault, and the plan was to attack simultaneously North of the Carentan Estuary, and between that and the River Orne, on the Normandy coast. The First US Army was to capture the Cotentin Peninsular, and the port of Cherbourg, while the Second British Army's task was to protect the left flank of the Americans. Assaulting between Port en Bessin and the River Orne, the British Army Commander, Lieut. General M. Dempsey, planned to secure a bridgehead South of the line St Lo — Caen. This was to be done on a two-Corps front, with 30 Corps on the right, and 1 Corps on the left.

Airborne landings were to be made on both flanks of the Army Group front during the night before D Day, and the seaborne forces would assault early on D Day.

The 30 Corps Commander's plan was to assault the localities of Le Hamel and La Riviere, and then to secure the high ground South of the beaches, and South East of Bayeux.

For this operation 30 Corps had under command the 7th Armoured Division, the 49th and 50th Infantry Divisions, the 8th Armoured Brigade, and elements of the 79th Armoured Division, together with the 47th Royal Marine Commando, whose task it would be to capture Port en Bessin and the coast defence battery at Longues. The assault was to be made by the 50th Division, and the 7th Armoured Division would follow up at last light the same day, while the 49th Division was scheduled to land four days later.

Concentration of the Corps troops had been completed by the end of May, and its Divisions spread along the coast from Harwich to Southampton.

Extensive reconnaissance of the invasion area had, of course, to be made before the landing was attempted, and low-flying aircraft of the RAF had taken photographs from many angles of the German under-water obstacles. The enemy based great hopes on these metal erections, which, he expected, would tear the bottoms out of our landing craft before the occupants could get ashore.

The Germans had, all along, been quite convinced that any attack along the coast would be put in on the Pas de Calais area. Consequently, while the Pas de Calais itself was strongly defended, the coast of Normandy had been very much neglected. The possibility of an attack here, evidently, began to be realised early in 1944, and in February Rommel ordered the construction of under-water obstacles, strong points, and batteries, and the mining of the beaches. A period of feverish activity followed, and it was seen from air photographs that defences were appearing in great numbers. It was rumoured, however, that progress was not fast enough to satisfy Rommel, and to appease the Commander on one of his visits, danger signs were erected where mines should have been, but actually were not.

In a letter dated May 22nd Field Marshal Rommel expressed his appreciation. "The main defence zone on the coast is strongly fortified and well manned," he wrote. "There are large tactical and operational reserves in the rear areas. Thousands of pieces of artillery, anti-tank guns, rocket projectiles and flame throwers await the enemy; millions of mines under water and on the land lie in wait for him. In spite of the enemy's great air superiority, we can face coming events with the greatest confidence."

A few weeks before D Day a sample of beach texture in the invasion area was obtained by a particularly daring reconnaissance, and it was found that some of the beaches had strips of soft blue clay, which might cause serious bogging of vehicles. A geologically similar beach was found in Norfolk, and the 79th Armoured Division was given the task of finding an answer to this last-minute problem. The answer was found, and a number of tanks were fitted with coir carpets, or "Bobbins", which could be laid over the soft patches.

For the first time in the history of seaborne assaults it was intended to put the armour ashore even before the infantry had landed. To do this all tanks and vehicles had to be specially waterproofed so that they could drive off the landing craft through six feet of water. In addition Sherman tanks had been fitted with certain technical modifications enabling them to swim off from a landing craft under their own steam, and be navigated by their commanders to the shore. These "DD" tanks, as they were called, could be launched from a distance of anything up to 7,000 yards out to sea, although the operation became dangerous in rough weather. For the invasion several armoured regiments were equipped with these tanks.

It had been intended to launch Operation "Overlord" on June 5th, but weather conditions imposed a delay of 24 hours. Even then the experts could hold out no hopes for the weather we so much desired, but with part of the forces already afloat, with spirits high, and with the prospect of a month's delay if the plunge was not taken, it was finally decided to invade.

That day a memorable personal message was sent to the troops by General Montgomery. He said:

> "The time has come to deal the enemy a terrific blow in Western Europe. The blow will be struck by the combined

sea, land, and air forces of the Allies — together constituting one great Allied team, under the supreme command of General Eisenhower. On the eve of this great adventure I send my best wishes to every soldier in the Allied team. To us is given the honour of striking a blow for freedom which will live in history; and in the better days that lie ahead men will speak with pride of our doings. We have a great and righteous cause. Let us pray that the 'Lord Mighty in Battle' will go forth with our armies, and that His special providence will aid us in the struggle. I want every soldier to know that I have complete confidence in the successful outcome of the operations that we are now about to begin. With stout hearts, and with enthusiasm for the contest, let us go forward to victory. And, as we enter the battle, let us recall the words of a famous soldier spoken many years ago: —

> 'He either fears his fate too much,
> Or his deserts are small,
> Who dare not put it to the touch,
> To win or lose it all.' "

For many weeks the Allied airforces had been engaged in the task of isolating the battle area. Bridges over the Seine and the Loire had been under constant attack, and many had been destroyed. Eight out of the nine railway bridges across the Seine between Paris and the sea had been smashed, and attacks had been constantly made on the main road bridges. Consequently any effort to reinforce the German troops in the invasion area would be seriously hampered. On the night of the 5th the weight of the air attack was switched to the German coastal defences, and by moonlight early on June 6th the airborne drop was made.

In the darkness of that night the landing craft set off. The weather was none too good, for there was a heavy swell in the Channel, and a strong wind blowing. The seaborne troops had an uncomfortable time, and breakfast was not a popular meal aboard the ships. Few of the men had any sleep during the crossing, many of them were sick, and the rough seas, sweeping in-board had soaked them. For all that the sight in the grey dawn of June 6th was an inspiring one. The sea was covered with Allied vessels of every description ranging from battleships and destroyers, to flak ships and minesweepers, with hundreds of landing craft of every size and description.

Men of the assaulting infantry of 30 Corps transferred from the larger ships to the small assault boats which would carry them to the beaches. Meanwhile fighter-bombers were roaring overhead in reassuring numbers, and the big guns of the Navy were pumping shells into the enemy's positions, while rocket craft were laying a carpet of destruction across the beaches.

Flail tanks of the 79th Armoured Division, with their revolving chains, went in to clear lanes through the minefields for the following infantry and tanks, while special armoured vehicles dealt with the under-water obstacles, and DD tanks, in support of the infantry, prepared to follow up. The rough sea made the launching of these very precarious, and many did not reach the shore. A squadron of the Sherwood Rangers Yeomanry was to provide covering fire for the infantry of the 50th Division. The original intention was to launch them some 7,000 yards out, but the heavy seas made it necessary to get closer to the shore. The enemy were becoming more active with their shelling and some of the craft were hit.

Lieutenant Stuart Hills MC was commanding a troop of tanks in C Squadron. The ramp of his landing craft had just been let down when a shell landed on the side of it, and another close by, wounding Sergeant Sidaway. Lieutenant Hills decided to launch immediately, but as soon as they entered the water it was apparent that something was wrong. Water poured into his own tank everywhere, and it was evident that the first. shell had holed one of the bottom plates. It was hopeless to try and save it, and the crew scrambled into their rubber dinghy. A few seconds later the tank, "Bardincollis", disappeared under the waves. Things were going badly for this troop, as not far away two other tanks were going down. Naval craft picked up Lieutenant Hills and his crew, and treated them to a welcome breakfast of whisky and Mars Bars. They could not be put ashore as this craft was too busy bombarding the beaches with a six pounder and twin Oerlikons. The next day they borrowed a dinghy, and made a rather belated invasion of the continent in this.

In some cases, however, the launching of these DD tanks was more successful. The tanks of the 13th/18th Hussars were launched from 5,000 yards out, and most of them reached the beaches safely to support the 3rd British Division on our left flank. The sight of tanks swimming ashore from deep water considerably startled the Germans.

The 1st Battalion, the Dorsetshire Regiment, the left assault Battalion of 231 Brigade, landed a little to the East of Le Hamel at half-past seven. There was a considerable amount of shelling and mortaring, but it was not until they advanced inland that really stiff fighting began. The other assault Battalion, the 1st Hampshires, met with opposition in Le Hamel itself, and from the beach defences West of it.

Le Hamel was still holding out in the afternoon, and then AVREs, (Assault Vehicles Royal Engineers), mounting petards, were put in to support the Hampshires in the street fighting. The well-known landmark, the sanatorium, had been turned into a strong point by the enemy, and received attention from one AVRE under the command of Sergeant Scaife, who fired two petard "dust-bins" at it. The infantry then assaulted, and took 20 prisoners.

The most important objective from the Dorsets' point of view was the hill about a mile inland, known as Point 54, which dominated the beaches and contained a battery position and strong points. C and D companies, under the command of Major RM Nicholl and Major WN Hayes respectively, assaulted with great dash and determination and overcame the first of these defences, suffering considerable casualties. The advance was frequently held up by heavy and accurate fire, but both the company commanders showed great determination and courage by continually reorganising their men, and pressing the attack. Both these officers were later awarded the Military Cross.

A Company, under the command of Major AAE Jones completed the capture of the chief strong point, killing many Germans and taking a large number of prisoners. By that evening the Battalion had reached all its objectives although casualties had been very heavy and many of the best junior leaders, officers and other ranks, had been killed or wounded. The attack was supported by a squadron of the Sherwood Rangers.

The 2nd Battalion, the Devonshire Regiment, third battalion of the Brigade, passed through to capture the village of Ryes. At the entrance to the town two large craters were found, which completely blocked the road. Men of 295 Field Company, Royal Engineers, used their tanks as bulldozers, and crashed a diversion round them, thus enabling the attack to proceed. The good people of Ryes were very anxious to know if this was merely a raid, or the real thing at last. On being assured that it was indeed the real thing, their delight knew no bounds, and bottles which had long been stored for this occasion quickly made their appearance.

69 Brigade, with the 6th and 7th Battalions, the Green Howards, and the 5th East Yorks made the landing to the West of La Riviere. Tanks flailed paths for the infantry, and a large crater on the road to Vers was quickly bridged. After assaulting across the beaches, the company commander of D Company noticed that two pillboxes had been bypassed by the leading platoons, and in company with CSM SE Hollis, he decided to inspect them to see that they were clear. They approached to within twenty yards of one of them, when a machine gun opened fire from it. The CSM, completely disregarding his own safety, rushed straight at the pillbox, firing his Sten gun as he went. He leaped on to the top of it, recharging his Sten, and threw a grenade

D DAY. MEN WADING ASHORE FROM THE LANDING CRAFT ON 30 CORPS' BEACHES

in through the door. He then fired his Sten into it, killing two Germans, and the remainder surrendered.

He captured several Germans from a nearby trench, and by his gallant action he undoubtedly saved his company being fired on from the rear and enabled them to clear the beach.

The sea wall was giving protection to German infantrymen who were engaging our men with machine guns and grenades. Captain DA King RE charged the wall with his AVRE, crashed over it and routed the enemy.

Tanks of the 4th/7th Dragoon Guards followed up swiftly from landing craft to support the assault. One of them, making its way along the beach to the exit, was held up by a broken-down Jeep. As no time could be wasted the tank drove straight on, crushing the Jeep, much to the annoyance of its owner. The tanks soon made contact with the Green Howards, and began to push inland, meeting a few Boche infantry in a brisk encounter which gave them the opportunity of warming up their machine guns.

In Crepon men of the 6th Green Howards encountered a field gun with its crew armed with Spandaus, and were held up. CSM Hollis, previously mentioned, was put in charge of a support group to cover the attack on the gun, but the attack could not make headway. Seeing this, the Sergeant-Major pushed forward to engage the enemy with a PIAT from a house only 50 yards from them. He was grazed by a sniper, and the field gun then fired into the house at point blank range. To avoid the falling masonry, he moved to another position, and shortly afterwards the gun was destroyed.

Discovering that two of his men were still in the demolished house, he went forward with a Bren gun, and, although he was under constant fire, he engaged the enemy until the two men got clear. For his unparalleled gallantry throughout this day CSM Hollis was awarded the Victoria Cross.

The advance was held up at Creully, where the Germans flooded the area, and the only road forward was well covered with fire. Typhoons were called in, and the enemy was forced to retire. Snipers were troublesome, but were finally dealt with, and the advance went on against stiffening opposition.

Men of the Royal Electrical and Mechanical Engineers (REME) landed with the first waves, and quickly established beach recovery sections and workshops. The workshops, formed from 30 Corps Troops Workshops and 7th Armoured Troops Workshops, with certain specialist personnel attached, were capable of dealing with all types of equipment. The beaches were under fire and for the first 48 hours they worked without a break under most unpleasant conditions.

A particularly gallant action on the part of one of the REME was that of Corporal RR Gale of 25 Beach Recovery Section, who cleared a blazing ammunition lorry from a beach exit. He was subsequently awarded the Military Medal. REME had contributed substantially to the success of the assault landing and the subsequent build up.

By that evening on 30 Corps front seven safe exits through the minefields had been made by the flail tanks, and were clearly marked. As a result of the heavy fighting in Le Hamel all the D Day objectives had not been obtained, but by nightfall the leading troops of 30 Corps had penetrated about five miles inland from the beaches, and on the right they were only two miles from Bayeux. On the right flank the 47th RM Commando had reached a point three miles from Port en Bessin, after a stiff fight at La Rosiere.

21 Panzer Division had put up a hard fight against 1 Corps on our left, but the airborne landings had been successful, and the 6th Airborne Division had obtained a bridgehead over the Orne River.

On the right the US forces had not used any specialized armour, and there were heavy losses in the rough seas. Their infantry landed first, without tank support, and by nightfall they had penetrated inland only a short distance, suffering heavy casualties. Unfortunately, by a freak of coincidence, the Germans were holding anti-parachute exercises in this area, and consequently the enemy was better prepared than had been expected.

The invasion had gained a great tactical surprise, and it was obvious that the enemy still could not be sure whether this was the real thing, or whether it was only a diversionarv effort. The main attack was still expected in the Pas de Calais area, and this prevented the enemy moving any reserves from this area until it was too late.

The long awaited D Day had come and gone, and the famous Club Route was open again. As the Prime Minister, Mr Churchill, stated in the House of Commons on June 6th, the defences of "Fortress Europe" had proved less insurmountable than had once been expected.

Rommel evidently still had the utmost faith in his defences, for when the invasion began he is reported to have said, reassuringly, "There will be no fighting on land, only on the beaches".

As D Day closed the beaches presented a scene of great activity as more men and supplies were landed, and the wounded and prisoners were taken off. Dukws, which had arrived early in the day loaded with ammunition, were used to carry our casualties to the tank landing craft. One of these Dukws, heavily loaded with casualties, broke down during the four mile journey to the bigger craft that night, and drifted for seven hours before being rescued.

Resistance was lighter on the Corps front the next day, and by noon our troops had taken all their D Day objectives. Port en Bessin and the coastal battery at Longues were taken by the Commandos with 200 prisoners, and during the afternoon the 50th Division encircled Bayeux. This old Norman town was found to be undefended, and was entered during the day.

A bridge over a railway cutting near the town was found to be blown and No 2 Platoon of the 295 Field Company RE went forward to deal with it. With the assistance of bulldozers the cutting was completely filled, and a 40 feet wide road constructed. The local inhabitants enthusiastically paved a strip 18 feet wide, but the remarks of the people who arrived later to get the railway working, and had to remove the huge pile of earth, had to be heard to be believed.

The third brigade of the 50th Division, the 151st Infantry Brigade, consisted of the 6th, 8th, and 9th Battalions of the Durham Light Infantry.

Major GC Wells MC RA, commanding a battery of the 90th City of London Field Regiment, which was supporting the 9th Battalion, the Durham Light Infantry, in an attack on an objective South of Bayeux, was making a recce for an OP to cover the Battalion zone. The only suitable place was the roof of a large barn. This not only provided a suitable OP on the roof, but gave them a pleasant surprise on the ground floor. The large room was packed with crate upon crate of Champagne, soap, boot polish, and a hundred other types of Boche stores.

On June 7th the 7th Armoured Division, the first complete armoured division to land in France, started to disembark.

Although no enemy tanks had yet been seen on the Corps front, 1 Corps on our left was engaged in a fierce battle against German armour of the 21st Panzer Division. On the right the Americans were now going ahead well after their initial difficulties.

The extension of the bridgehead continued against stiffening opposition and on the following day the 8th Armoured Brigade, with the 1st Dorsets acting as its motor Battalion, thrust forward to seize the high ground South of Bayeux. The enemy's intention was evidently to seal off the bridgehead, and he was making determined efforts to hold the important road and rail centre of Caen by armoured counter attacks, and 1 Corps was held up in this area. Our own thrusts South towards Tilly-sur-Seulles were strongly contested. On the right flank of our bridgehead the

50th Division was engaged in bitter fighting for the town of Sully, which was not taken until the 9th.

For the first time tanks were met on the Corps front, and several were knocked out. The 8th Durhams, with tank support, reached St Pierre, North East of Tilly, and all the ground North of the Bayeux — Caen road was finally cleared. On the right the Americans captured the little port of Isigny, and a link up was made with our troops at Sully.

On June 10th the 7th Armoured Division took over a portion of the front from the 50th Division, and began to attack towards Tilly. The close Bocage country, with its many sunken roads and leafy lanes, was favourable to the enemy infantry, and our tanks found the going difficult as it was possible for the infantry to hurl grenades from close range and snipe through the open turret hatches. That night, in spite of the difficulties, the armour had taken Bernieres Bocage, and reached the North West outskirts of Tilly.

All this time the big guns of the Royal Navy had been supporting our troops as they fought their way forward. Battleships, cruisers and monitors took part in these co-operative shoots, and a typical message sent to the Naval flagship on June 10th read: "30 Corps requires one of your biggest chaps to help them all tomorrow. Good sport promised."

By June 11th, the 2nd Gloucesters, of the 56th Independent Brigade, under command of 50th Division, succeeded in establishing themselves on the cross roads in Tilly, but the position was precarious. The Panzer Lehr Division made continual counter attacks throughout the day, and that evening our troops were forced to withdraw.

To the North of Tilly the 1st Dorsets were counter attacked by tanks. The fighting was intense, and casualties high Stretcher bearers behaved gallantly under the difficult conditions. One of them, Private R. Goddard, continued to look after the wounded even after he himself was wounded. His persistent courage won for him the Military Medal.

To the West of Tilly a Battalion of the 56th Brigade, the 2nd Essex, was having a hard time of it in the area of the Verrieres Wood. For hours the Battalion fought against Tiger tanks and infantry, unsupported except by artillery. The area was being flooded by enemy artillery and mortar fire, and when the German flame throwers came in our men could be seen dashing from cover to cover in an effort to evade being burnt alive.

Screams of a man from somewhere near the enemy position were ignored at first as it was thought to be merely a Hun trap to get our men to go forward and investigate. The Commanding

Officer, Lieut Colonel Higson MC, and Major MW Holme, believing it to be one of their own men, crawled out in the direction of the weakening screams, and returned an hour later with a horribly burned and wounded man. Unfortunately their brave action was in vain, for this man died before reaching hospital.

Sherman tanks in use as Artillery OPs had been modified for the job by having the 75 mm guns removed, and a piece of appropriately painted tin piping inserted to resemble the gun. By doing this there was more room inside the turret for technical gunnery work.

Captain JPR Bland of the 90th City of London Field Regiment was the OP officer of a battery in support of the 6th Green Howards attacking towards Cristot on June 11th. Strong opposition was encountered, and Captain Bland found numerous targets for his battery and his regiment, particulars of which he sent through on the wireless set in his turret. Hard pressed infantrymen quickly noted that this particular tank was not taking its share in the firing, and Captain Bland had to endure a number of disgusted criticisms: "Why the Hell don't you fire your so and so gun"? and "Why don't you fire, that's what the so and so gun's for, isn't it"?

Rather exasperated, Captain Bland moved the Sherman forward amidst loud cheers, to do his best. But worse was to come, for the only weapon he had was a 30 Browning, and when the troops heard this instead of the healthy bark of the 75 mm which they had expected, the cheers turned to jeers. To add insult to injury, the signaller raised his hatch at that moment to see what was going on. The burst from the Browning shot away the periscope, frightened the signaller badly, and scattered ricochets round in all directions. Captain Bland then gave up trying to be a tank, and concentrated on his proper job of finding targets for the real guns. Amicable relations with the infantry were not resumed until they were let into the secret of the bogus gun.

On the right the Americans were making excellent progress and heading for Caumont. Taking advantage of this, it was decided to pull 7th Armoured Division out from the hard fighting in and around Tilly, and they were directed to put in a right hook attack, with the object of capturing Villers Bocage from the West.

During the night of June 12th the Division pulled out, and went through the American sector to within about three miles of Villers Bocage. At dawn the move was continued, and the town was entered by the 4th City of London Yeomanry with very little opposition. For two hours things were peaceful, and then a number of enemy tanks were seen entering the town. A and HQ Squadrons quickly became involved, and although they fought very gallantly against hopeless odds, they were both completely written off. The Commanding Officer was captured, and the Second in Command killed, and Major Aird, the former leader of B Squadron, took over command of the Regiment.

Subsequently it transpired that these attacks were made by the 2nd Panzer Division, which was passing through Villers on its way further North, and the surprise of armour meeting armour was mutual. A troop of Cromwell tanks of the City of London Yeomanry, commanded by Lieutenant Cotton, edged its way towards the centre of the town. Turning into the main street, the crew of the leading tank, commanded by Corporal Horne, saw a German Mark IV Tank 20 yards away, while behind were two alert Tiger tanks, the foremost of which started to swing its gun to engage them. Trooper Wood, the gunner, quickly shot up the Mark IV, which burst into flames, and the driver, Trooper Grimshaw, reversed the tank into a side street with commendable celerity.

The German tank men dismounted to peep round the wall at the British tank, and a game of hide and seek began. Armour-piercing shells were fired at our tank through the intermediate buildings, fortunately without effect. The crew noted the words "Justice et Paix" on a battered building with mixed feelings.

After a time the Huns seemed to consider that our tank had been knocked out, and one of the Tigers started up. As the hull appeared at the end of the street, Trooper Wood fired one shot which put the tank out of control, and it crashed into a building. One Tiger tank remained to be dealt with.

In the meantime the troop commander, Lieutenant Cotton, had entered a house overlooking the Tiger. Seeing that the tank was shut down, and that there was no sign of activity, he assumed that the crew had baled out. He collected some petrol, poured it over the tank, and was about to set it alight, when, to his surprise, the tank moved off. Once again Corporal Horne was on the alert, and dealt with it in the same way as it crossed the end of his street.

By this time fierce battles were going on all over the town, and men of the Queens Royal Regiment had arrived to play their part with six-pounder anti-tank guns. The enemy were on all sides, and at one time an OP officer of the 64th Medium Regiment RA found himself engaging targets which were between his own position and the guns. About five o'clock in the afternoon it was realised that the opposition was too strong, and a withdrawal was made to a high feature West of the battered town.

Meanwhile French Resistance activity was coming up to expectations. Railway sabotage was widespread, particularly in the South and West of France. In the South East road traffic had been severely interrupted. The Resistance Movement had undoubtedly contributed to the delay in getting reinforcements to the battle area from the South. Further, German troops had to be left to cope with the Resistance Groups, and it was reported that a part of the 2nd SS Panzer Division had been diverted to deal with the situation in Central France.

By the night of the 15th no less than 11,000 prisoners had been taken on the Army Group front, and the bridgehead was extending slowly but surely. During the day an attack was launched on the village of Lingevres, West of Tilly, by the 9th Durhams, supported by tanks of the 4th/7th Dragoon Guards. The attack, which was preceded by aerial bombing, and a barrage by the Corps artillery, went well, and the village was taken.

Then, however, the enemy reacted violently, and put in a strong counter attack, supported by armour. A terrific tank battle ensued at close quarters, during which one particularly good bag was secured by Sergeant Harris of Salisbury. With only five rounds from his 17-pounder he knocked out five Panther tanks, and was later awarded the Distinguished Conduct Medal for his gallantry and skill. The situation eased, the remaining German tanks pulled out, and Lingevres was firmly in our hands.

By the evening of June 15th the first phase of Operation Overlord was completed. By now the 21st Army Group had secured a good bridgehead, supplies were coming in satisfactorily, and it looked as if it was quite impossible for the enemy to dislodge us. However, he was doing his best by denying us the use of the ports of Cherbourg and Caen, but in the meantime, we had built our own port at Arromanches, the famous Mulberry. Heavy casualties had been inflicted on the twelve divisions which had been thrown in against us, and with our air and sea superiority, the future looked bright. 30 Corps alone had been responsible for the destruction of 70 of the enemy's most modern tanks.

On June 16th the most important advances were made by the Americans on our right who, by capturing Montebourg and St Saveur le Vicomte, were now more than half way across the neck of the Cotentin Peninsular. General Montgomery's intention, all along, had been to draw enemy reserves on to the Second Army's front, making it easier for an American break-out, and the success of this was now becoming apparent. A number of bitter actions were going on all along the British front against the best troops the Germans had in the area.

The 49th Division cleared the fortified villages of Bronay and Cristot on the 16th, the latter being taken by the 1st/4th Battalion, the King's Own Yorkshire Light Infantry, whose first action it was. They were supported by a heavy artillery programme, which included guns of the Royal Navy. The villages were heavily booby trapped, an enemy policy which had been met with frequently, and even crucifixes and dead bodies were used as traps for our men.

On the evening of the 17th the 9th US Infantry Division reached the coast at Portbail, thus cutting the Cherbourg Peninsular in two. It was estimated that approximately 34,000 troops were now cut off in Cherbourg and the area around the port.

By the 18th the battle for Tilly, which had been waged incessantly for nine days, was almost at an end. Troops of the 50th Division were on the North and West of the town, while troops of the 49th Division were on the East. During the encirclement of Tilly, a company of the 7th Battalion, the Green Howards, attacked a strongly held farm. The enemy waited until they were within short range, and then opened up with heavy mortar and machine gun fire. The company commander and 20 men were pinned down, and became non-effective. Lieutenant FS Lawson, a platoon commander, gathered the remnants of the company together, and led an attack on the farm. After fierce fighting in which there were heavy casualties on both sides, the enemy surrendered. Lieutenant Lawson, who had previously rescued a badly wounded NCO under fire, was awarded the Military Cross for his gallantry and leadership.

By three o'clock on the afternoon of the 19th Tilly was captured, and the 50th Division reached the outskirts of Hottot. Once again many booby traps were found in Tilly.

During the attack on the town troops of the 2nd Battalion, the Essex Regiment, were held up by heavy fire. One particularly effective Spandau was cleverly sited in the edge of a wood, and its exact position could not be located. Lieutenants Filby and Vince crawled forward, armed with Sten guns, and with a camouflage jacket tied to a long pole. They exposed the jacket to draw fire and betray the position of the gun, but for twenty minutes nothing happened. They thought that the Germans must have gone, but on moving less cautiously, received a quick burst of fire. Evidently the Germans were fully alive to the ruse, and the officers returned slightly discomforted to their troops.

During the next few days there was little change in the position along the Corps front. On our right flank the Americans reached the perimeter defences of Cherbourg, and on June 21st the German garrison was given an ultimatum to surrender, which was rejected, and it was not until the 26th that the city and port were captured.

During this time landing operations on the beaches were held up by a big storm, which lasted from the morning of the 19th to the evening of the 22nd. The mountaineous seas caused considerable damage, and washed up enormous masses of wreckage on to the beaches. The whole of the 43rd Division, and many other troops of the follow up element were compelled to remain on the storm-tossed ships much longer than they wished.

Meanwhile the British 8 Corps had arrived in the bridgehead and taken up a position in the line between 1 Corps and 30 Corps. They were given the important task of seizing crossings over the River Odon South West of Caen, and immediately before they began, 30 Corps was to attack to secure the area of Noyers.

Soon after four o'clock on the morning of the 25th our divisions began the attack supported by the 8th Armoured Brigade, with the 49th Division on the left, and the 50th Division on the right. In the opening hours of the attack there was a very thick ground mist which hampered operations but when the mist cleared good progress was made by the 49th Division, which captured the village of Fontenay le Pesnal. On the right 50th Division, meeting more resistance, made some ground South of Tilly.

Resuming the attack the next morning, tanks of the 8th Armoured Brigade supported men of the 49th Division in a thrust towards Rauray. Although the enemy fought hard, and opposed our advance with many tanks, resistance was gradually overcome, and by the evening a foothold was obtained in Rauray, although the village itself was not cleared until the next day.

A squadron of the 49th Reconnaissance Regiment was protecting the left flank of the Division during the advance to Rauray. They crossed the Fontenay — Cheux road, and became engaged with a number of enemy Panther tanks. The Recce men unlimbered their six pounders, and a brisk fight took place, as a result of which three German Panther tanks were brewed up, and a German Mark IV Special tank was knocked out. The squadron was able to take the ground they had been ordered to hold, and they remained there for the next five nights without seeing any more German tanks.

The 8 Corps' attack was going well, a bridge over the Odon a mile South of Mondrainville was secured intact, and two battalions of infantry and two regiments of tanks established themselves on the South side of the river. The next day they strengthened their bridgehead in spite of counter attacks by the 2nd SS Panzer Division. This division had been rushed from the American sector to meet the threat of the new British attacks.

Few advances were made on the following days, the enemy putting up a determined resistance in all sectors. In particular the fighting around Brettevillette was very bitter, and the village changed hands several times.

The important road centre of Villers Bocage was heavily bombed by aircraft of Bomber Command on the night of June 30th. 250 planes took part in this attack, and a total of over 1,300 tons of bombs was dropped. As a result of the raid Villers was completely flattened, and all roads blocked, thus adding to the chaos of German communications in this area.

By the end of June General Montgomery's plan to attract the German armour to the British front had succeeded, and the Second Army was holding all the German armoured divisions. On the Normandy front huge casualties had been inflicted on the Germans, and since D Day they had lost over 90,000 men. Further, 360 tanks had been put out of action by the Second Army, and of these 30 Corps could claim the destruction of more than one third.

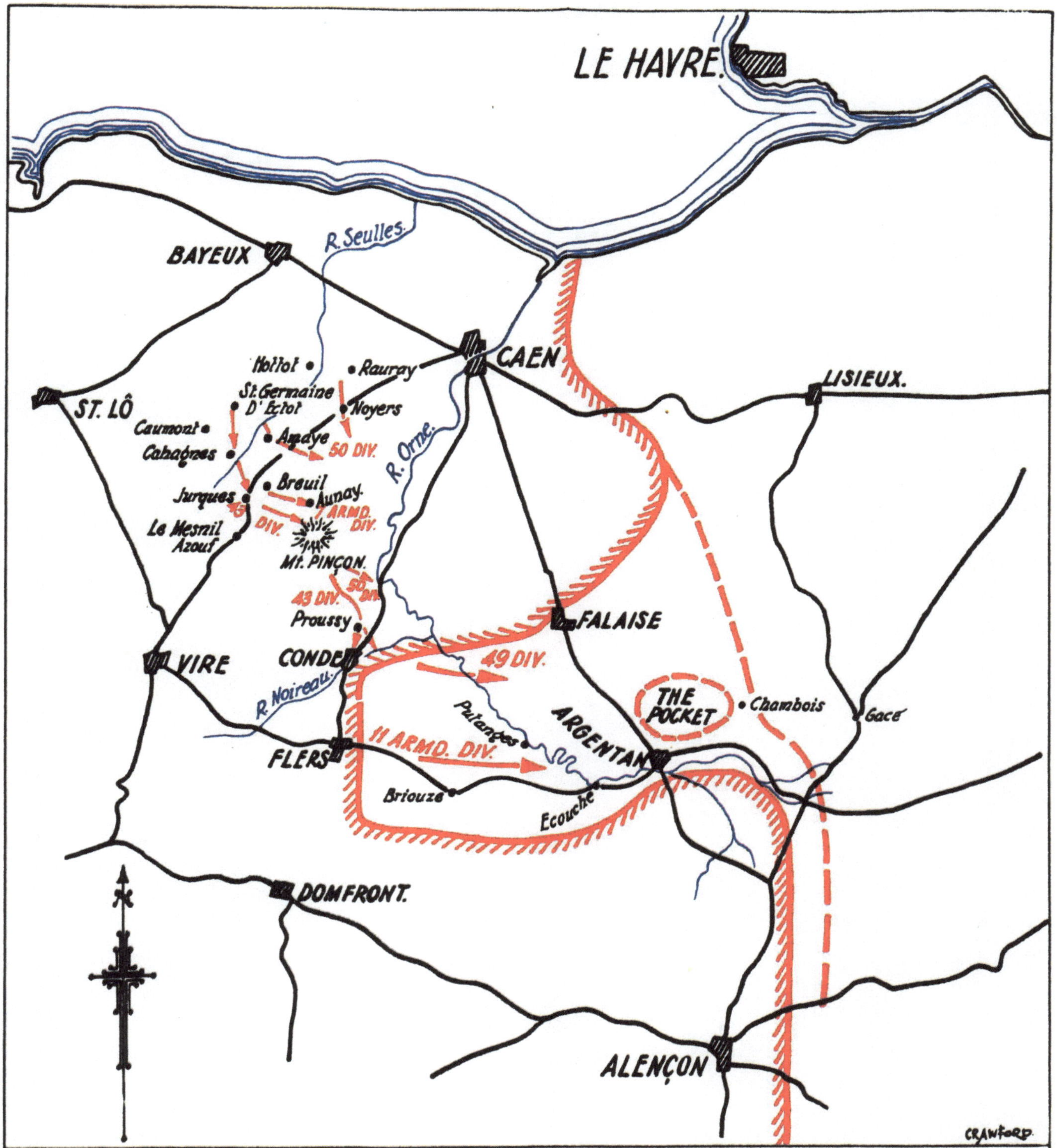

THE BOAR CHARGES.

LINE AT 16 AUG.

LINE AT 19 AUG.

SCALE 1: 750,000.

10 5 0 10 20 30 40

• Miles •

CHAPTER TWO

THE BOAR CHARGES

Rommel's boast that there would be no fighting on land, only on the beaches, had been proved an empty one, but the German commander had not given up his attempt to drive the invading forces back into the sea. The great mass of German armour opposite the Second Army front made its presence felt during the early days of July, and a series of vicious counter attacks were launched against our positions from Caen to Caumont.

The young Nazis of the well-trained Panzer Divisions flung themselves against the British troops, and bitter fighting took place, especially on the 30 Corps front.

The most serious of the counter attacks were those put in against the 49th Division in the Rauray area, and during July 1st no less than four were repulsed. Under cover of a smoke screen, just before seven o'clock in the morning, strong armoured thrusts were launched, but the men of the 49th Division held their fire until the Tiger and Panther tanks were quite close, and then did great slaughter. In an area of about half a square mile over 30 enemy tanks were knocked out.

From nine o'clock onwards the enemy attacked determinedly, and it was not until four o'clock in the afternoon that he gave up the attempt to break through our obstinate defences, and by this time he had suffered heavy losses, and our positions were still intact. The fighting was fanatical, and on more than one occasion an enemy sniper, who was cornered, committed suicide rather than allow himself to be captured. To add to the confusion of the battle our men were, in some cases, using captured Spandaus.

Excellently co-ordinated artillery fire played a large part in the breaking up of enemy concentrations, and repelling the attacks. The Corps Artillery was, in fact, obtaining a domination over the enemy's batteries which it was seldom to lose in the future.

At this period the 5th US Corps took over the sector which had been held by the 7th Armoured Division, and our armour went into Army Reserve. For the next two days the German troops on the Second Army front were content to lick their wounds, and the Corps front was comparatively quiet. Another German infantry division, the 276th, made its appearance in the line after a very uncomfortable journey from Bayonne. For six unhappy days it received full attention from our fighter bombers, and thereafter had to travel by night. All hope of rail travel was abandoned at Le Mans, and the warriors continued their journey to the battle front by bicycle and on foot.

About this time 213 Field Ambulance opened its first Advanced Dressing Station in the battered village of Cheux. The operating theatre gleamed with polished chromium, and the most scruffy of orderlies looked angelic in a spotless white gown. Everyone stood and admired it. Then the shells came. In half a minute the place was a shambles, the operating theatre was just dirt and plaster, the blood transfusion room had disappeared, and the ambulance unloading point was a hole in the ground. It took only fifteen minutes to get the ADS organised again, but it was not an object of admiration like the first. However, it did excellent work, and in the next 36 hours 400 patients were dealt with.

Meanwhile the Americans had cleared all the Cherbourg Peninsular North of the Cotentin — St Sauveur line, and were pushing slowly but steadily Southwards. By the 8th of July they had captured Le Haye de Puits, and enemy armour was being withdrawn from the British front to meet this new threat. On the same day 1 Corps, on the left flank, began an attack on Caen. This was preceded by a terrific air bombardment which did irreparable damage to the old Norman port.

At the same time 30 Corps attacked with the 50th Division in the area of Bois St Germaine, and by the evening the 56th Infantry Brigade had reached the Caumont — Caen road. In the newly won territory Sergeant Stannard and a party of six men of the 149th Field Ambulance, including Sergeant Chippendale MM, were looking at a farm house with a view to taking it over as an ADS. When they entered the kitchen they found six German officers seated at the table, who made them welcome, and pressed them to stay with the aid of their Lugers.

One of the officers spoke tolerable English, and began to ask them how many British soldiers were in the area. Sergeant Stannard told them that the British were all around them. The Germans then had a lively conference in their own language, at the close of which the English speaking one announced that a bargain was to be made. The party of Englishmen must give their word of honour to stay where they were for an hour, while the Germans made their getaway.

This was agreed upon, and away went the German officers. The delighted ambulance men watched through the farm window as they walked straight into a patrol of the Green Howards, and were made prisoners themselves.

By July 9th the greater part of Caen had been cleared by 1 Corps, and the bridge over the River Orne was captured intact. It was here that the first of the enemy's swimming saboteurs was encountered. A German Naval Officer was taken out of the water after a fruitless attempt to blow the bridge.

This was not the first time that Caen had been captured by the British, for in 1346 King Edward III with his son the Black Prince landed at St Vaast la Hogue. Their progress was rapid, and capturing Carentan, St Lo, and Fontenay le Pesnal, they arrived at the gates of Caen on July 26th, only 14 days after their landing. At this time Caen was considered to be a larger city than any in England except London. Welsh troops swam the river, and outflanked the enemy who finally surrendered.

Counter attacks on the Corps front were now directed against our newly won positions in the 50th Division's sector. Timely warning of the attacks was given to us by an enemy deserter, and once again they were broken up by artillery fire and the staunchness of our infantry. This prisoner was not one of the braver types. His philosophy was: "It's no use any more. I've noticed that everyone who fires cops it. Me and my mate, we don't let off a single shot. We're not as stupid as all that."

The Americans were now across the River Vire, and were approaching the important town of St Lo. 12th Corps on our left attacked on July 15th and seized Gavrus, and on the following day the 59th Division, which had joined 30 Corps on the 13th, gained a footing on the high ground South of Brettevillette. Two days later men of the 2nd/6th South Staffordshire Regiment of this Division fought their way into Noyers.

On the same day at dawn the heaviest and most concentrated air assault ever launched in support of a military operation heralded the Second Army's offensive from the bridgehead over the Orne. Over 2,500 heavy bombers and 600 mediums blasted a gap 7,000 yards wide through the main enemy defences, and a powerful armoured and infantry attack was launched by 8 Corps through this gap. Three armoured Divisions, the 7th, the 11th, and the Guards smashed their way Southwards, advancing nearly seven miles by midday. Fearful of being outflanked by this onslaught, the enemy made a series of withdrawals on the 30 Corps front, and the 50th Division, taking advantage of this opportunity, followed up the withdrawal rapidly, capturing Hottot, and taking 300 prisoners.

A captured German report said: "The Allies are waging war regardless of expense. They have complete mastery of the air; they bomb and strafe every movement; they recce our area constantly and direct their artillery fire. Against all this the German Airforce is conspicious by its absence."

Field Marshal Rommel, the German commander against whom 30 Corps had been opposed since the early African campaigns, was wounded about this time. The driver of his car was hit by a bullet from a strafing aircraft, and the car turned over. Rommel received a fractured skull, and retired to Germany where he died in October.

On July 18th the enemy rallied and checked the armoured advance, but a good pivot had been gained by the Second Army on which the Americans could swing Southwards and Eastwards, and begin the break-out from the bridgehead. The next task of the British Army was to attack the enemy South of Caumont, and prevent him using the high ground of Mont Pincon as a pivot for withdrawal in face of the Americans.

Accordingly a certain amount of regrouping took place on the Second Army front, and the 43rd Wessex Division now came under the command of 30 Corps for the first time. The Corps was directed to advance Southwards from Caumont on July 30th and seize the Mont Pincon feature. The 50th Division, the 8th Armoured Brigade, and the 7th Armoured Division were also under command, the latter in reserve.

Heavy clouds hampered the air attack which preceded the main assault, but our aircraft came down almost to zero feet, and nearly 4,000 tons of bombs were dropped on the enemy. Progress on the Corps front on this first day was limited as the enemy had laid mines thickly, and booby traps were plentiful. Better progress was made on the second day, when the 43rd Division cleared the enemy from Cahagnes, and captured intact two bridges South of the town. By the evening the 1st Worcesters of 214 Brigade were advancing against slight opposition. The Northumbrian Division captured St Germaine d'Ectot and Orbois. On our right 8 Corps had reached the Foret l'Eveque and La Ferrieres, while further right again, the Americans, by capturing Avranches, were now prepared for a break out on a big scale.

On the next day the 7th Armoured Division was brought into the battle, and attacked towards Aunay sur Odon, reaching Breuil by that evening, but meeting hard resistance. The 43rd Division, after a day of heavy fighting, managed to scale the slopes of the Bois du Homme feature, and knocked out 12 German tanks.

During the night elements of 130 Brigade, riding on the tanks of the Sherwood Rangers Yeomanry, pushed on towards the village of Jurques, which was entered in the early hours of the morning. The 214 Bde occupied the high ground South of Jurques near Mesnil Auzouf as a flank protective force after the DCLI had engaged a strong German rear-guard of tanks and infantry. It was from here that Lieut. Stock MC of the 5th DCLI, disguised as a French poacher with a bag of ferrets, penetrated the enemy lines and brought back valuable information and a big, surly German CSM. Jurques had received a very heavy hammering from the RAF, and not a house was standing. Many detours had to be made round the badly cratered roads, and the advance was delayed by the inevitable mines. Leaving the 7th Hampshires to hold Jurques, the 4th Dorsets and the tanks pressed on to La Bigne.

Approaching the village the enemy held them up with intense machine gun fire, and Lieutenant Hills took his tank forward. Rounding a corner, he was confronted unexpectedly by three enemy tanks at short range, one of which he knocked out. Then began a game of hide and seek with the other two among the trees of an orchard.

The right flank of this column was exposed to the enemy who were holding the high ground to the South, and the Germans brought up tanks to enfilade the road. These however were kept at a distance by the accurate shooting of the Sherwood Rangers, who brewed up several enemy tanks.

The enemy mortaring was very intense, and the infantry suffered heavily, but by midday the village was taken. A conference which was held shortly afterwards by infantry and tank officers was brought to an abrupt end by the arrival of a mortar bomb, which unfortunately inflicted many casualties. Conferences in La Bigne that day were not a success. At another one that night the house in which it was held received a direct hit, and was set on fire.

Meanwhile infantry of the 50th Division had got into Amaye and pushed towards the line of the River Seulles.

Men of the 43rd Reconnaissance Regiment were experiencing the thrill of going into action for the first time. The ship carrying them to Normandy had been sunk, and while the infantry of the Division were fighting their first battles with 8 Corps, they had been reorganising in a rear area. It would be difficult to describe the individual feelings of a Reconnaissance troop in their first operational role. The five armoured cars, and seven Bren carriers making up the troop, move along in bounds in front of the infantry. Somewhere they will meet the enemy, but how and when is unknown. Perhaps there will be no warning until an 88 mm shell arrives.

C Squadron of this Regiment carried out its first operation probing in front of the Division on August 2nd, from Jurques along the approaches to Mont Pincon. Driving down the once beautiful Bois du Homme, the troops passed the remains of a German horse-drawn transport column which had been caught by our artillery. When they reached Le Mesnil Auzouf they found that the Germans had already left. They had a delighted welcome from the villagers, but there was no time for celebration, and they soon pushed on. One troop went on for several miles without meeting any enemy, but then they came to a signal wire looped across the road. After looking for mines, the troop commander, Lieutenant IM Davies, cut this wire, and immediately a hail of mortar shells fell around the troop.

Meanwhile the assault troop, commanded by Lieutenant Richardson, had taken over a village on a crossroads in the rear of the leading troops. Owing to heavy mortaring they were forced to abandon it, and the troop commander was wounded. When darkness came, the forward troops were ordered to withdraw, driving through the blazing village in the twilight. Their first recce had come to an end, and a deep penetration of enemy territory had been made without a German being seen.

The next two days saw continual counter attacks, which were all repelled. Aunay was finally captured on August 5th by the 7th Armoured Division, the 11th Hussars finding the town a shambles of bombed buildings and cratered roads.

The business of opening routes through the town was a serious one, for rubble was everywhere, and it was difficult to see where the actual streets had been. Men of the 209 Field Company, Royal Engineers, of the Corps Troops Engineers, were given the task of producing routes either through or round Aunay. Without Bulldozers the task would have been almost insurmountable, but with their help lanes were cleared, and the traffic was able to make its way through. In the first 24 hours this Company cleared 1,500 yards of street, and created some 2,000 yards of diversion routes.

Meanwhile the Americans had broken into the Brittany Peninsula and their armoured columns were sweeping Westwards almost unopposed. Rennes was taken, and the Germans were forced to fall back into the coastal fortresses of Brest, St Malo, Lorient, and St Nazaire. The German commander tried to cheer up his troops, according to prisoners' statements, by telling them that great masses of troops and tanks were on their way to the Normandy battle area, and that the Allies would be thrown back into the sea within 60 days.

The 43rd Division, partnered by the 8th Armoured Brigade, was now ordered to capture Mont Pincon. This dominating

BRITISH TANKS PASS A KNOCKED-OUT TIGER IN A LANE NEAR TILLY-SUR-SEULLES

feature, 1,200 feet high, lies in the so-called "Little Switzerland" of Normandy. It stood athwart several roads essential to the advance, and there were no illusions as to the difficulty of assaulting this hill, for its slopes were steep, and it had long been prepared by the enemy as an important key point, and the German defenders were deployed in strength with many machine guns sited on the wooded slopes.

On the afternoon of August 6th, 129 Brigade began the assault, in the heat of a cloudless summer day. The enemy had complete observation, and was able to mortar the infantry with great accuracy. The infantry were pinned down by the vicious fire, but tanks of the 13th/18th Hussars, using splendid initiative, gained the crest of the hill. The sight of the tanks on the hilltop acted as a tremendous spur to the infantry, and men of the 4th Somersets, and the 4th Wiltshires, determined to support the tanks, moved up the hill in the failing light, and cleared the well established enemy positions.

An important part in the capture of Mont Pincon had been played by the 7th Battalion, the Somerset Light Infantry, who put in a diversionary attack down the main road towards Roucamps. By doing so they drew the attention of a whole German Regiment, thus easing the task of the main attacking forces.

The loss of Mont Pincon was a serious blow to the Germans, and it was expected that they would try to recover the position, but for some reason no counter attack developed.

Next morning an officer of the 7th Somersets, who would probably prefer to remain anonymus, was standing on Mont Pincon. A voice hailed him from behind: "Have you seen the Corps Commander?" Without turning he exclaimed: "Good Heavens, you don't expect to find him this far forward, do you?" He then turned, and to his embarrassment he found that he was talking to a Major General.

But the Corps Commander was, in fact, on Mont Pinçon that morning. Private Pursey of the Anti-Tank Platoon failed to notice the badges of rank, and called out to him: "Got any 'gen', sir?" Lieut General BG Horrocks, CBE DSO MC did have some "gen", which he shared with the small group which quickly gathered.

The 5th Battalion, the Duke of Cornwall's Light Infantry, made a feint attack down the road with a Squadron of the 4/7th Dragoon Guards and one platoon of Riflemen. The Battalion moved swiftly along the Southern slopes of Mt Pincon, surprising the enemy. They knocked out a Royal Tiger Tank, killed 30 of the German Infantry and captured 120 of them for the loss of only five men. They then pushed on and during the evening cleared Le Plessis Grimoult.

By August 8th the Americans had reached Le Mans in the South, but further North were being heavily counter attacked in the Mortaine region, where five Panzer Divisions were attempting to break through to Avranches. Success here for the enemy would have meant cutting off the American armour, which had burst out through this neck to swarm over Brittany. However the Allied airforces quickly got to work on the enemy's armoured columns, inflicting terrible losses on them, and the attack was stopped.

An interesting sidelight on Prussian mentality can be gained from the following extract from a captured German order.

> "Again and again I meet soldiers in the Department Eure who, as cyclists, do not keep their legs stiff when saluting. This is against orders, when the bicycle is freewheeling, and the journey is not uphill. I request that all units be informed."
>
> (Signed) Gollnitz Col District Cmdr.

Even when the German Armies in the West were on the point of annihilation, one had to keep one's legs stiff when saluting on a bicycle.

Shortly after midday on August 9th the 50th Division took up the attack on the Corps front, and by last light had reached the high ground East of Grapouville. The enemy still resisted strongly, although the jaws of a trap were closing behind him, for the Americans, moving fast, were approaching Alencon, and the Canadians were closing on Falaise. For the next three days the Northumbrian Division made dogged progress towards Conde sur Noireau, and every day a few more hard-won kilometres were gained.

In the 5th East Yorks casualties were high, and in one case Corporal Grace was the only section commander left in his platoon. He showed excellent leadership, and utter disregard for his own safety, and when one of his men was wounded later, Corporal Grace dashed across open ground, covered by snipers, and rescued him. For his courage and resolution he was awarded the Military Medal.

On August 13th the 50th Division was withdrawn, and the 43rd Division once more took on the chase. The 7th Somersets were advancing toward Mont Gauthier, and the Pioneer Platoon, which Lieutenant D Bean commanded, was clearing the road behind the leading company under heavy shellfire. Lieutenant Bean worked calmly with a Polish mine detector all the time, and when this job was finished, he went forward to see if he could help the leading troops, who were being counter attacked. Picking up a Bren gun, he chased the enemy when they started to run. On his way back to Battalion Headquarters he found a wounded man in a ditch. He began to dress his wounds under shellfire, and suddenly a batch of mortar bombs landed all around them. Lieutenant Bean threw himself on top of the wounded man to protect him. He was successful, but suffered severe shrapnel wounds himself. For this brave action he was awarded the Military Cross.

On the following day Proussy was captured, and our troops got to within two miles of Conde. The Regimental Aid Post of the 5th Battalion, the Dorset Regiment, was established in a barn near Proussy, in which there were a number of cider barrels. Every night someone's chocolate or food disappeared, and there was a good deal of ill feeling, until after three nights a shadow was seen between the barrels and the wall. On investigation a German soldier was found hiding there. He was very scared, and so weak from lack of food that the padre had to climb over and help him out. The mystery of the vanishing food was explained.

It now became clear that the enemy had seen his danger, and was pulling back on the Second Army front. Addressing a message to his troops, General Dwight D. Eisenhower, the Supreme Allied Commander, said:

> "Through your combined skill, valour, and fortitude you have created in France a fleeting, but definite opportunity for a major Allied victory, one whose realisation will mean notable progress towards the final downfall of our enemy. In the past, I have, in moments of unusual significance, made special appeals to the Allied Forces it has been my honour to command. Without exception the response has been unstinted, and the results beyond my expectations.
>
> Because the victory we can now achieve is infinitely greater than any it has so far been possible to accomplish in the West, and because this opportunity may be grasped only through the utmost zeal, determination and speedy action, I make my present appeal to you more urgent than ever before.
>
> I request every airman to make it his direct responsibility that the enemy is blasted unceasingly by day and by night, and is denied safety either in fight or in flight.
>
> I request every sailor to make sure that no part of the hostile forces can either escape or be reinforced by sea, and that comrades on the land want for nothing that guns and ships and ships, companies can bring them.
>
> I request every soldier to go forward to his assigned objective with the determination that the enemy can survive only through surrender; let no foot of ground once gained be relinquished, nor a single German escape through a line once established.
>
> With all of us resolutely performing our special tasks we can make this week a momentous one in the history of this

war — a brilliant and fruitful week for us, a fateful one for the ambitions of the Nazi tyrants."

On August 14th the 11th Armoured Division came under command, and 30 Corps was given the task of pursuit, being directed to push forward as quickly as possible to Argentan.

The Germans withdrew across the shallow little River Noireau with the 7th Somersets on their heels, and a patrol of that Regiment, led by Captain JW Baden and Pioneer Sergeant Martin set off to reconnoitre crossing places for the Division. The patrol made its way down a sunken lane without incident, and then left its shelter to cross the meadows down to the river. They quickly spotted a German sentry on the far bank, but fortunately he was not looking in their direction, and they reached the sunken lane again without being seen. Under cover of the hedge they reached a small village where they met a young French workman, who gave them valuable information about the river crossing. From the windows of a mill they were able to survey the river bed, and could see Gemans digging in machine gun positions on the far bank. Taking advantage of the overhanging bank they took off their boots and steel helmets, and paddled the stretch of stream in which they were interested. Whether the Germans saw them or not, they did not interfere, and the reconnaissance was satisfactorily completed.

Their only wish now was to get back while the going was good, but the villagers had other plans. They were not allowed to go before being toasted in cognac, and photographed with one of the village girls — all this with the Germans not 200 yards away.

That night the men of the 214th Brigade of the 43rd Division got across the river opposite Conde, and the 11th Armoured Division crossed and reached the Flers-Conde road. By now German transport was thronging the roads, providing fine targets for the Allied airforces, and the gap was steadily closing.

The armour advanced rapidly, overcoming pockets of paratroopers, still stubbornly fighting, and reached Briouze, where they made contact with the Americans. They then pressed on to Putanges, and cleared the woods at Ecouche, thus further compressing the enemy pocket. On the 19th our troops were across the Orne at Putanges, where a bridge had been completed, and drove on beyond Sentilly.

On the same day the Falaise Pocket was finally closed when the Polish Armoured Division of the Canadian Army linked up with the 5th US Corps at Chambois. The trap was sprung, and the killing ground encircled. By day and by night the Allied airforces and artillery pounded away without mercy at the remnants of the German Seventh Army.

All attempts by the enemy to break out, and all attempts to break in to rescue the trapped divisions were frustrated, and the destruction of the encircled troops went on. The pleasant leafy Norman countryside was turned into a scene of carnage and destruction, as the German troops fought on in their useless struggle to escape.

The German 3rd Parachute Division, which was trapped in the pocket received a stimulation order from its commander "It is rumoured that the Division is encircled . . . . The army, British or American, which can encircle or capture our division does not exist . . . . It is certain that we will finish this war victoriously . . . . Whosoever thinks or speaks differently will be slapped across the face."

A captured letter from one of the Germans trapped there to his home gives a vivid picture of the terrible conditions inside the encircled area. The writer seems to have escaped.

> "I was in the Argentan-Falaise pocket, and I still don't know how I got out of it. We were running in wild fiery circles with artillery and aerial bombs dropping amidst us. After I got out of there I had to fight partisans and our own soldiers to get on to the ferry across the Seine. Just accidentally I met my old battery again, after having been on my own for ten days. Naturally it is very euphemistic to call whatever is left a battery. There is not even one gun left."

Falaise will long be remembered as the scene of one of the greatest military disasters in history. More than 3,200 German vehicles, tanks, and guns of all types were destroyed, and the German army in the West was utterly crippled.

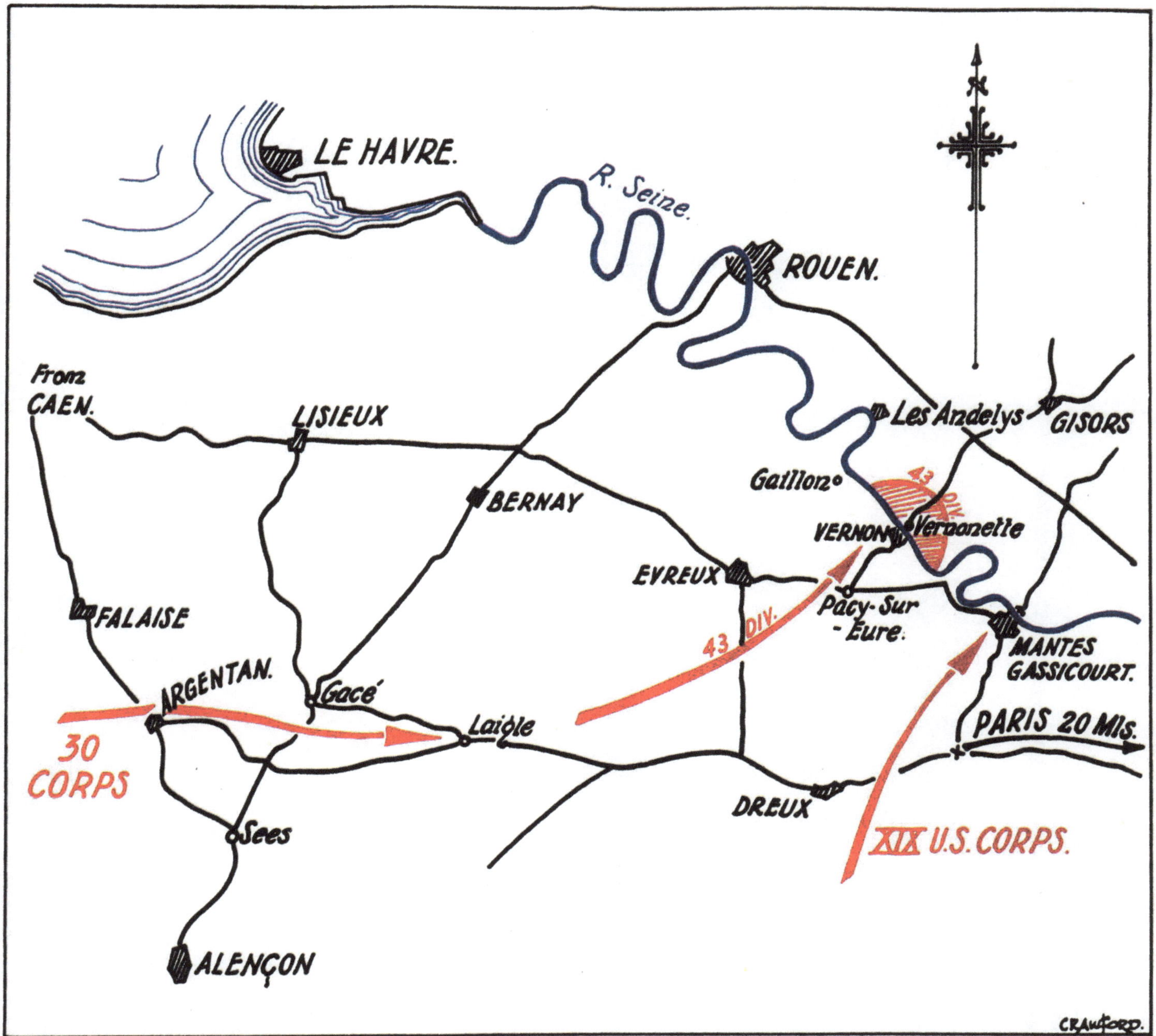

ACROSS THE SEINE.

0 10 20 30 40
· Scale of Miles ·

CHAPTER THREE

ACROSS THE SEINE

Enemy resistance in the now famous Falaise pocket finally ended on August 22nd. About 70,000 German troops had been killed or captured, and those who had been successful in escaping from the gap were now in full retreat across the Seine.

General Sir Bernard Montgomery sent a personal message to his troops, which began:

> "On the 11th of August I spoke to the officers and men of the Allied Armies in NW France. I said we must 'write off' the powerful German forces that were causing us so much trouble; we must finish it, once and for all, and so hasten the end of the war.
>
> And to-day it has been done. The German armies in North West France have suffered a decisive defeat; the destruction of enemy personnel and equipment in and about the so-called 'Normandy pocket' has been terrific, and is still going on; any enemy units that manage to get away will not be in a fit condition to fight again for months; there are still many surprises in store for the fleeing remnants. The victory has been complete, definite and decisive."

Meanwhile, the 79th US Division of the 19th US Corps had reached the Seine and established a bridgehead at Mantes Gassicourt. This they were steadily enlarging, despite the frantic efforts of the enemy to reduce it. Advancing on Paris from the South, the French Armoured Division and American infantry were meeting only slight resistance, while in the Capital itself, citizens, members of the Resistance Movement FFI and Gendarmes were fighting pitched battles with the Germans. Paris was finally liberated on August 25th, and the city wildly celebrated the end of its four and a half years of German occupation.

With the growing confidence of the French population, resistance activities increased everywhere. In areas by-passed by the rapid advance of the Allied Armies, FFI men were rounding up Germans from the countryside and handing their prisoners over. They were able, too, to patrol the roads and guard lines of communication. Sabotage was being maintained on a high level, and many of the railway lines had been severed, thus crippling the German sources of supply.

There was an occasion when a German Battalion Commander was found to be missing, and although the Huns searched in all directions and turned villagers, out of their houses and cross-questioned them, only the Commander's car was ever found. The FFI, evidently, were trying their hand at yet another form of sabotage.

The Second British Army, with 30 Corps on the right and 12 Corps on the left, advanced to the Seine. With the 50th Division on the left flank, the 11th Armoured Division continued to drive forward towards the river, passing through Argentan and Gace, and entering L'Aigle on August 22nd.

During this rapid advance, several enemy pockets were by-passed, and Battery Sergeant-Major J Anthony, of the 90th City of London Field Regiment, RA, attached to the 50th Division, who had been compelled to drop out of the convoy owing to a puncture, was riding his motor-cycle along the route beyond Argentan when a Frenchwoman stopped him and told him there were Germans only a few hundred yards down the road. She directed him back to Argentan by another road, but he was stopped at the village of St Christopher by a party of FFI men who had kept track of his movements for several miles by a system of 'bush telegraph' which they had invented.

They took him down into a cellar and showed him their armoury. He met many of the members, including a number of girls, and then they directed him on to L'Aigle. When he arrived there he found that Americans and Germans were fighting in the town, and that his own unit was not there. He returned along the same road, and came upon a German tank which had just broken down. He shot past it at high speed, and eventually caught up with his Regiment. He had traversed about 68 miles of occupied territory, and brought back with him much useful information.

The advance gave Traffic Control many unexpected problems. One indignant military policeman left his post and walked into the nearest Brigade Headquarters.

"Look here," he demanded heatedly, "how can I control the ruddy traffic when a Tiger tank keeps coming up and shooting at me?" His particular problem was quickly dealt with and the Tiger tank duly knocked out.

The 43rd Wessex Division was given the task of being the first British Division to assault the Seine, and reconnaissance parties dashed forward to Vernon. They were temporarily delayed by a bridge over the River Eure at Pacy, which the Germans had blown. A forward RE officer had discovered, further, that it was mined, blocked and booby-trapped, and that the only troops in the vicinity consisted of one solitary US Military Policeman. Engineer parties, including men of 30 Corps Troops RE, escorted by a troop of the 43rd Reconnaissance Regiment, moved forward to bridge the gap and clear the mines. They found that, beyond the river bridge, the crossing of the road over the railway was also demolished.

At this stage a party of US Engineers arrived from the far bank, also with orders to bridge the Eure, but an international compromise was reached, and our men built the river bridge, while the Americans bulldozed a crossing over the railway through the station yard. In the early hours of August 25th, the leading troops entered Vernon without incident.

The pleasant, straggling town of Vernon lies extended along the Western bank of the River Seine, the woods and buildings giving a good covered approach to the river. On the other side of the river, opposite the town on a narrow strip of flat ground, is Vernonette. Immediately behind, and on either side of Vernonette, the ground rises in an escarpment which completely dominates the river and both banks. The upper parts of the escarpment are covered with woods which extend Eastwards from the river for about five miles.

The Germans on the far bank had been accustomed for some days to the presence in Vernon of elements of US Reconnaissance units. As far as was known, they were not anticipating any attack, and in order that surprise should be complete, strict orders were issued by Major General G I Thomas, CB DSO MC, that no British uniform or British steel helmet was to be seen on the river bank prior to the assault. These limitations did not in any way prevent a most detailed reconnaissance being carried out by all branches of the 43rd Division. During the afternoon, a complete machine-gun company of the Middlesex Regiment was brought into position in rooms overlooking the far bank. A squadron of the 15th/19th Hussars fixed positions near the bank for their guns and Besas. Observation posts were occupied by the gunners, assembly areas for boats, rafting gear, and assaulting battalions, were reconnoitred and sign-posted. All this was done without an inkling reaching the enemy of what was afoot.

The operation was planned for the night of the 25th, the speed of the attack preventing the Germans from reinforcing their defences there. The assault was mounted from a point 120 miles away from the West bank of the river, and the leading infantry of the assaulting brigade, the 4th Somersets and the 4th and 5th Battalions of the Wiltshire Regiment, were carried over the last 90 miles in Dukws. An intense quarter of an hour barrage was put down against all the known enemy positions on the cliff-like opposite bank. Then, at seven o'clock in the evening, under cover of a smoke screen and only two hours after arriving in their operational area, the assaulting troops were launched.

The crossing was a hazardous one, for the German gunners had full observation, and, moreover, the banks were steep and muddy. A large number of weeds fouled the propellers of the Dukws and assault boats, exposing the men to the heavy fire of the enemy. The 4th Battalion, the Somerset Light Infantry, landed on what was in effect an island, as a wide water course which had been thought to be dry proved to be filled with water, and was consequently impassable. The troops of the Battalion were, later, re-embarked. The 5th Battalion, the Wiltshire Regiment, was landed with difficulty upstream of the town, and was counter-attacked when only one company was across. However, the remainder of the Battalion got over in the early hours of the morning, and were joined at first light by the 1st Battalion of the Worcestershire Regiment, who crossed dryshod by the demolished road bridge and advanced towards Vernonette.

During the morning, in order to create doubts in the mind of the German Commander as to the exact location of our main crossing places, two ruses were used. Ostentatious registration by the RA with high explosive and smoke was carried out up and down the river, and a small party, consisting of one 25 pounder with 100 rounds of smoke, a 3 inch Mortar, and a carrier section, was sent out to go some 15 miles downstream and simulate a landing opposite Gaillon.

At midday, the 4th Battalion, the Wiltshire Regiment, also crossed. By this time enemy opposition was being overcome, and the Royal Engineers had assembled a Class 9 bridge, but all their efforts to swing it across the river were frustrated by machine-gun fire from the far bank. Anti-tank gunners and lighter vehicles were ferried across the river by rafts in spite of the enemy fire.

The Engineers completed the construction of this 680 feet bridge by six o'clock in the evening, and reinforcements with vehicles and Bren carriers crossed immediately. The bridgehead was now firmly secured, and, by that night, we held an area 1,000 yards deep and 5,000 yards wide. Work was now started on a Class 40 bridge, but considerable inconvenience was caused by the

THE CLASS 9 BRIDGE IN POSITION AT VERNON. ON THE LEFT THE CLASS 40 BRIDGE IS NEARING COMPLETION

breaching of a dam by the Germans downstream, which caused the level of the river to fall by six feet.

A tank ferry was brought into operation during the night of the 26th/27th, and early the next morning the first tanks of the 4th/7th Dragoon Guards, of the 8th Armoured Brigade, crossed the river. Probably the first British tank over the Seine was that of a troop leader, Lieutenant MAT Trasenster. The journey across was made without incident, but on reaching the far bank the ground was found to be much softer than had been expected, and the tank was quickly bogged. Representatives from the infantry battalions who had formed the bridgehead were waiting for tanks to get across, for enemy counter-attacks were being put in. The one bogged tank did not arouse their enthusiasm. However, a few more tanks of the Squadron were ferried across, and it was not long before the Class 40 bridge was ready. Then the rest of the Regiment streamed over and were quickly in action.

Lieut. Thomas, a troop leader in the 4/7th Dragoon Guards, with Sergeant Warrington, were detailed to contact a missing company of the Dorsets. They pushed on among the trees, and, following the sound of firing, came upon a party of British troops who had been captured. Warrington put his head out of the turret and shouted: "Hey, there! Make a break for it!" They gave covering fire and the troops dived for cover, but at this moment Sergeant Warrington was killed. Then, as the enemy fire was increasing, the remainder of the crew saw that they would have to get away. They got back to Headquarters, and here a counter-attack was quickly organised which proved successful, and the enemy was driven off.

Meanwhile, the Germans were making counter-attacks on the men of the Wessex Division. The 1st Battalion, The Worcestershire Regiment, while advancing up the main road, were strongly counter-attacked and driven back. Major Benn, the Second-in-Command, lost his life while rallying the leading troops. Major Algy Grubb and Capt. Noel Watkins massed all available Bren guns and the counter-attack was finally beaten off, but it had been an awkward moment.

At the same time the 7th Battalion, The Somerset Light Infantry, had an isolated Company surprised and destroyed in the Forest. On the left of the bridge-head, the 5th Battalion, The Duke of Cornwall's Light Infantry had a platoon over-run in a night attack. When Major Parker, MC MM, of A Company was in danger of a similar fate, he brought down the fire of the Divisional Artillery on to his own position and Company Headquarters, and broke up the attack.

By the 28th, the bridge-head had been extended to a depth

of four and a half miles. The speed with which the 43rd Division had secured the Vernon bridge-head was of the first importance in the continued destruction of the German forces. It was an operation which had been brilliantly executed.

Now the men who were to exploit this river crossing began to assemble. The leading troops of the 11th Armoured Division were already in the neighbourhood of Vernon, and the 50th Division had arrived in the area Southwest of it. The Guards Armoured Division, now under the command of 30 Corps, moved into the area of Laigle. An armoured break-out across the plains of Flanders would eliminate the "V" weapon sites in the Pas de Calais, from which the flying bombs were being launched on London and the South Coast.

Although Hitler had promised us only six of these "V" weapons, a civilian gave information of another one, about which nothing had been heard. He said that all the live rats in Normandy had been bought up by the Germans at the huge price of 100 francs a tail, and shipped off in small cages to be infected with typhus. Thousands of small parachutes would also be provided, and these diseased rodents would be dropped over England. It was anticipated that the rats would eat through the greased strings of the parachutes, and so be free to roam the countryside on their deadly mission of spreading disease for the Fuhrer. No doubt this tale was started by some German with an unexpected sense of humour.

Crippled by appalling losses and without satisfactory reserves, the German forces were in a parlous state. Eleven weeks of vicious fighting, culminating for the Germans in a blood-bath big enough even for their extravagent taste, had brought them to a stage where they could only make a shattered retreat across France to their own frontiers.

THE RACE THROUGH FLANDERS · I.

SCALE 1:1,200,000.

0 10 20 30 40 50 60 70 80

· Miles ·

CHAPTER FOUR

THE RACE THROUGH FLANDERS

Now the great chase across France began. The starting gate was up, and the Corps got away to a flying start, with two armoured brigades leading, the 8th on the right and the 29th on the left, both under command of the 11th Armoured Division. The 50th Division was to follow on behind the armour, while the Guards Armoured Division, which was still at Laigle, was to join in the chase at a later date.

30 Corps' task was to establish itself in the area of Arras — Amiens, regardless of the progress of the forces on its flanks. Now was the opportunity to push Club Route ahead at a rapid speed through the good tank country of Northern France, past the scenes of the battles of the first Great War. It was going to be a lone battle, for before long the Corps troops were stretched out far ahead of the flanking formations.

The advance went well on August 29th, the first day. Resistance, although still well organised, was confined to small bodies of infantry sited in villages and at road blocks, and, during the day, only three enemy tanks were seen. By nightfall, the 3rd Royal Tank Regiment and the 8th Battalion the Rifle Brigade had surrounded and taken Mainneville, having advanced 20 miles. On the right flank, the 8th Armoured Brigade, meeting more resistance, had reached a point about five miles from Gisors. As it seemed possible that the 8th Armoured Brigade might be held up, owing to strong opposition on the flank, the Corps Commander instructed Major General G. P. B. Roberts, the Commander of the 11th Armoured Division, to push on with his left column, which consisted of the 29th Armoured Brigade, and, consequently, on the next day a further 40 miles was covered by the tanks on the left hand route, and the leading armour of this Brigade was only 15 miles short of Amiens. The 8th Armoured Brigade entered

Beauvais that evening and found the bridges in the town intact.

By now, the Guards Armoured Division had come up on the right hand route and was preparing to pass through the 8th Armoured Brigade and continue the advance. The tanks on the left route pushed ahead through the night of the 30th/31st, and, at a quarter to seven in the morning, the message: "Forward troops have entered Amiens", was passed over the wireless to Corps Headquarters. The 3rd Royal Tank Regiment entered the town, much to the surprise of the German garrison. Fighting was going on between Germans and French Resistance men, and the latter had greatly aided our advance by saving the bridges across the Somme from demolition. By five o'clock in the evening, the last few enemy troops had been mopped up and the town was completely in our hands. 3,000 prisoners were taken by the 11th Armoured Division and the FFI, including General Eberach, the Commander of the German Seventh Army, together with his tactical headquarters.

Meanwhile, the Guards Armoured Division, which had left Beauvais in the early hours of the morning, had gone ahead almost unopposed. There was no longer any question of any more 'stands' or 'withdrawals to fresh positions' so far as the Germans were concerned, for their retreat had by now become an uncontrollable rout. Coming up level with the 11th Armoured Division, the Guards crossed the Somme to the East of Amiens, and, by nightfall on this amazing day, all the armour of both divisions was over the river.

The events of the last three days had been a welcome change for the men of the Corps after the slogging matches of Normandy. In three days, the Boar, with head down and hackles up, had covered 140 miles, completely surprised the enemy, and gained the crossings over the Somme. Three divisions, and one armoured brigade, were poised ready to push Club Route still further ahead.

Next morning, the Guards made for Arras, with the Welsh Guards and the 2nd Household Cavalry in the lead. They reached the town shortly after midday, having overcome stubborn resistance in Albert. The Germans had hastily formed what was known as the 'Somme Corps', and its Commander and his staff were captured in Arras by the 5th Guards Brigade. Pushing on, the armoured cars of the 2nd Household Cavalry entered Lens, and the tanks of the 2nd Irish Guards reached Douai. The 11th Armoured Division, meanwhile, encountering little opposition, had, by that afternoon, reached its objectives North of Arras.

The 11th Armoured Division had with them a mobile cinema unit from the 38th Kinema Section, but the advance was so swift that no chance was found to take advantage of any entertainment they might have provided. It was decided that the projectionists, Corporal Boswell and Private Bray, should return to their parent unit. Through a slight, but, as it proved, important error in map reading, they eventually landed up within shooting range of a party of Germans.

They decided to go away from that place. Guided by members of the Resistance Movement they set off rapidly back towards Arras. It was a ride which, in their opinion, put Dick Turpin amongst the 'also-rans'. On their way they had the honour, unwittingly, to liberate two villages. The villagers gave them a vociferous, if somewhat embarrassing, welcome, and invited them to stay for the rest of the war.

By a happy chance engine trouble, so they say, developed in the last village, but fortunately it was only a minor defect and three days later they were able to move on again. Slightly shaken, but with a good deal to talk about, they got safely back to their parent unit.

It may not be generally known that members of Civil Affairs were very often to be found in the front line, armed with only paste pot and poster. It was their duty to contact the local authorities and issue instructions for the preservation of order. With Major Macrae in command, such a detachment, consisting of four officers and six other ranks had already left Amiens and were making for Arras. All went well until they were within twelve kilometres of Arras, where they ran into a skirmish. As they were not fighting troops they decided to pull in to the side of the road, and the cook, adopting his favourite motto — "When in doubt, brew up" — made the usual tea.

They then pushed ahead, but were stopped by a gesticulating Frenchman at a bend in the road. Going forward to investigate, Sergeant B. Blackburn found one of the vehicles with the driver missing and the cook slumped on the seat, shot through the head. It was a sad day for Civil Affairs, for a detachment of ten is not a very big one, and the loss of two men is felt very considerably.

Meanwhile, the 8th Armoured Brigade, which was acting as left flank protection for the Corps, had captured Doullens. A squadron of the Sherwood Rangers Yeomanry was in the lead along the main road to Doullens, and was rather surprised to find itself in company with the Corps Commander. Lieutenant David Render, with the 5th Troop, was in the lead. He was about to go on when a girl ran up, weeping, who practically tried to push his tank back. She pointed up the road towards Doullens and cried, "Cannon! Cannon!"

The weeping was convincing and the squadron was ordered to deploy on a reverse slope to the left. One tank poked its nose over the top of the hill and immediately received a shell on the turret. Then Sergeant Dring, of the 3rd Troop, spotted a troop of cavalry some 2,000 yards away — an excellent target. The cavalry were quickly dealt with, and horses, men and supply wagons went in every direction, even upwards. Then another target presented itself in the shape of about two companies of infantry. As the tank guns opened up the Huns scattered into the neighbouring woods.

Two Spitfires dived down, but recognised them in time, and, circling round, engaged their targets without further delay. It was certainly an excellent example of air co-operation. The Southern outskirts of Doullens were reached after some anti-tank guns had been dealt with. Then, from the West, came a veritable Lord Mayor's Show. Three tanks appeared, with Sergeant Jackson's in the lead, and, riding on them, was a strange assortment of German prisoners, wearing most bizarre uniforms, many of them bedecked with gold braid. The squadron then pushed on, with 200 prisoners to their credit.

Following on behind, acting as Brigade reserve, were the 13th/18th Hussars. While Doullens was being attacked, it was thought that the enemy was escaping down the main road to Arras, and, to forestall this, some of the Hussars dashed round to cut them off. They found none of the enemy, but were spotted by a couple of Spitfires, which dived down to investigate. The pilots were evidently ten minutes out of date with the latest war situation, for they took them to be enemy tanks escaping from Doullens, and attacked. In fast mobile warfare of this nature, without the slightest indication of any front line, it was extremely difficult for our pilots to differentiate between friend and foe. On this occasion, Regimental Headquarters received their full attention, and most of the impedimenta on the backs of the tanks was written off. However, having taken stock, the Headquarters decided to live down this indignity, and moved on again.

The leading squadron found in a wood some bedraggled Germans, who emerged with arms raised. Captain P. C. C. Jury, the Intelligence Officer, disarmed them, and questioned the only NCO among them, who admitted that there were more Germans still in the wood. The NCO was told to go and fetch them out, and he shortly returned with another 30. This, he was told, was not good enough, and he was sent back again. He finally produced about 60, which, it was decided, was sufficient.

In the nearby village of Bouquemaison, meanwhile, an excited reception committee of French villagers was awaiting them. When the tanks entered the village they were quickly covered by swarms

MEMBERS OF THE FFI IN AMIENS AFTER THE ENTRY OF OUR ARMOUR

of small boys and girls, and the prisoners they had collected became mixed up with the enthusiastic villagers. Thinking that some might have escaped in the confusion, a check count was made. The prisoners were rounded up, and it was found that the number, rather astonishingly, had increased from 60 to over 100. It transpired that the new arrivals had been hiding from the FFI, of whom they were very much afraid, and they had taken this opportunity of joining the party.

The next day, a small boy riding a very tumbledown pony brought a note which read as follows:

> "To the Commander of the British Army.
>
> Sir,
>
> We ask at you of aid. The Germans are at the wood at St. Hougain, and they are at maybe 40 in number. We have three rifles only and one German gun, but no bomb, and they will not let us take them. We pray you to follow the rider to take them. Thanking you in anticipation. Vive Churchill."

But Brussels was calling and the regiment had to move off without accepting the invitation.

Early next morning, B Squadron of the 4th/7th Dragoon Guards arrived at Canaples, and rather unexpectedly ran into an 88 mm which opened up with a near miss on the leading tank. Lieutenant Simmonds, a troop leader, went forward on foot and located the gun, but could not get very near as snipers were covering it. Sergeant Perry, in the leading tank, dismounted to guide his driver to safety. He was hit and blinded in one eye by a sniper, but refused to give up until he had got his tank back under cover. His courageous action gained him the MM.

Meanwhile, another troop had discovered a Panther tank and brewed it up, after a cat and mouse struggle. They then went after the 88 mm and brewed up the half-track which towed it. The crew of the gun had decided that they would get hit sooner or later if they stayed where they were, and, unfortunately for them, they had just hitched up to the half-track when it was hit.

On the afternoon of September 2nd, the Corps Commander issued his orders to the Guards Armoured Division, and a conference was held at Divisional Headquarters that evening. The Divisional Commander, Major General Allan Adair, CB DSO MC, who had commanded the Division since Normandy, did not take long to give out his plan.

"My intention", he said, "is to advance and liberate Brussels. And", he added, "that is a grand intention."

Speed was essential, and any serious opposition would have to be by-passed. The Division would move on two centre lines, and the distance to be covered would in each case be about 90 miles.

The right centre line ran through Tournai, which had now been reached by the 1st US Army advancing on the right flank. At the same time as the Guards advanced, the 11th Armoured Division on the left would make a dash for Antwerp.

In the early hours of the next morning the Corps began the great advance, and astonishing progress was made by both armoured divisions. On the left, the 11th Armoured Division was hampered at first by enemy withdrawals from Lille, and the 50th Division was called upon to screen the exits from Lille and prevent the enemy interfering with the advance. With this opposition removed, the 11th Armoured Division moved on quickly, and that night arrived in the area of Alost.

The 73rd Anti-tank Regiment accompanied the 9th Battalion of the Durham Light Infantry to the outskirts of Lille, and one troop under the command of Lieutenant P. J. Clarke was attached to an infantry company in a little village near the town. The inhabitants produced a puny individual in ragged clothes much too large for him, and after a great deal of unintelligible conversation it was gathered that the puny creature was a Hun. He had come from a wood some 600 yards away, and he and his 200 mates wished to surrender. Unfortunately, however, they were commanded by a SS officer who was determined to spend all his ammunition before even considering surrender. It was decided to 'stonk' the wood with artillery, and a fifteen minute barrage was put in. Next day, the Recce people inspected the wood, and reported eight 105 mm guns knocked out, several others abandoned, and a large number of dead.

Meanwhile, on the right, the Guards armour had advanced smoothly, meeting only small pockets of resistance — 'poches de Boches', as one of their officers described them. The 2nd Household Cavalry Regiment had the difficult task of screening the two leading brigades, a task they fulfilled most admirably throughout the day.

The Belgian frontier was crossed at nine o'clock in the morning. The armour moved fast, the Resistance Movement men proving invaluable, not only in guarding prisoners, but also in clearing snipers and holding bridges. Local inhabitants, too, turned out with their spades to repair the roads where the tanks had turned.

At Mons en Pevele, the 90th City of London Field Regiment, which was part of the 231st Infantry Brigade Group, had the unusual experience, for a Field Regiment, of engaging the enemy over open sights. Two German columns were spotted, approaching from different directions. The batteries deployed in crash action

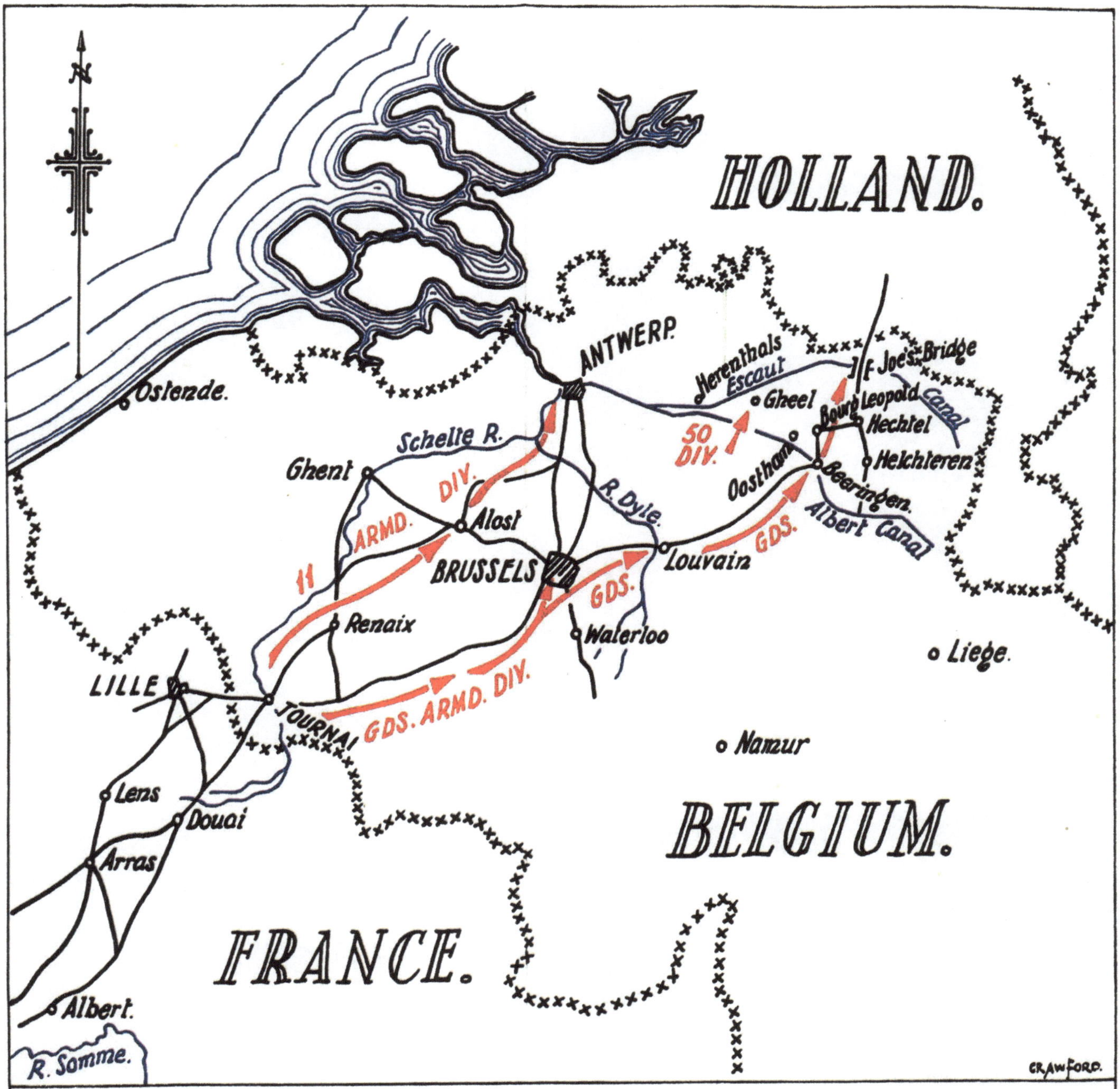

THE RACE THROUGH FLANDERS · II.

SCALE 1:1,250,000.

0 10 20 30 40 50 60 70 80

· Miles ·

and had a most satisfactory shoot, resulting in one 88 mm and ten vehicles destroyed, 15 Germans killed and 100 taken prisoner.

There was considerable friendly rivalry between the two Guards Brigades as to which would be the first to reach Brussels — a rivalry that increased as the distance to the Capital grew less. At a quarter past seven that night, the 32nd Guards Brigade reported its leading troops only two miles short, but at eight o'clock, the 2nd (Armoured Recce) Welsh Guards reached the winning post, having had a clear run at the finish. At the same time, the 1st (Motor) Grenadier Guards entered the outskirts of the city and effectively dealt with the anti-tank screen blocking the way.

The chief impediment to progress in the famous old capital was provided by the inhabitants themselves, who swarmed over everything and everybody in hilarious welcome. It was a magnificent reception, and no better day could have been picked for it, for it was the fifth anniversary of the start of the war.

Of the enemy there was little to be seen. A small party of them was found in hiding near the Palace and quickly dealt with. Patriots helped to mop up isolated pockets, but, apart from these minor incidents, the entry into Brussels was more like a triumphant procession than a battle.

Not a great deal of damage had been done to the city, except for the famous Palais de Justice, which had been set on fire by the Germans, and that night the Belgians continued their festivities by the light of the flames and the full moon.

The next morning, 30 Corps Headquarters entered the city through the madly cheering crowds and established itself in the Parc Royal. The Corps Commander took the opportunity of paying his respects to the Queen Mother.

The famous golf course at Waterloo, where Henry Cotton used to hold sway, and which was now a Black Market centre, was taken over by 2nd (Armoured Recce) Welsh Guards, who had won the race to Brussels, as their headquarters.

The Commander of the Guards Armoured Division drove past the tomb of The Unknown Warrior in his command tank, escorted by his troop of Cromwell tanks and a troop of the Household Cavalry.

Then came the Belgian Brigade, returning in triumph to their lovely capital. The crowds were so dense that it was only with difficulty that the procession was able to keep on its course. Flags, long hidden, appeared in every house and every hand, and the tanks were soon hidden under the showers of streamers and flowers. The Divisional Commander called to pay his respects to the Burgomaster in the historic Hotel de Ville.

A sharp reminder that, in spite of the celebrations, the war was not yet over, was given by some German 88 mm guns in the Foret de Soignes, which fired airbursts into the city. The crowds temporarily scattered, but no-one was hurt, and the celebrations went on. It was a moving tribute by the people of Brussels to the Allies, and a wonderful welcome to their own troops.

Meanwhile, the Grenadier Group made a welcome return journey to Louvain, whence they had been driven four years before. They captured the town, seized intact the crossings over the River Dyle, and renewed many old acquaintances. The 50th Division, who were protecting the rear left flank, entered Renaix, and sent an infantry brigade forward to protect the exits from Brussels.

At Renaix, information was received from the local Resistance Movement that the nearby village of La Pierre was strongly held by about 1,000 Germans, with a colonel in command. A troop of the Sherwood Rangers Yeomanry under the command of Lieutenant Wharton went to the village under the protection of a white flag, and demanded the surrender of the garrison, but the German colonel refused to discuss anything with anybody but an officer of equal rank.

Lieutenant Colonel S. D. Christopherson, DSC., MC., took B Squadron and a company of the 12th Battalion, the King's Royal Rifles, into the village. They travelled in a civilian car which had to be pushed by the locals before it would start, which rather detracted from the dignity of the occasion. The colonel took with him his Second-in-Command, Major Stephen Mitchell, who spoke a little German.

Their demand for surrender met with a cold response, the German Commander declaring that he considered himself strong enough to continue the fight. As he had a thousand men and an unknown amount of artillery against only one squadron of tanks and one company of infantry, he was probably quite right. However, after a long discussion, he agreed to surrender, and it was arranged that at seven o'clock that evening the Germans would rendezvous at the point in the village where the railway crossed the road.

At the time appointed, however, at the point where the railway crossed the road, there was no sign at all of the German garrison, a state of affairs that was rather disturbing. At half past seven, firing was heard on the far side of the village, and it afterwards transpired that there was another point in the village where the railway crossed the road, and here the Germans had been patiently waiting all the time. Unfortunately for them, however, a Battalion of the Green Howards had come face to face with them, and opened fire. The mistake was discovered before much damage had been done, and the German colonel was eventually placated. He then explained the incident to his troops, whose discipline throughout had been remarkable. In view of the misunderstanding that had occurred, the German colonel's request that his men might be allowed to break their rifles was agreed to, and the surrender was concluded satisfactorily.

The Corps SP Regiment, the 86th Field Regiment, was moving up through Tournai when one of the guns broke down and had to be left behind. Shortly afterwards it was repaired and the crew set off to catch up with the column. Some partisans, however, stopped them, and reported machine gun fire coming from a nearby wood. Already, they said, seven of the local inhabitants, and two RAOC men, had been killed.

Sergeant Telling investigated, and decided to put in an attack. Backed by a party of partisans, the crew advanced in line towards the wood, and, at thirty yards range, opened fire. Then, leaving two men to guard the tank, Sergeant Telling led the charge on the wood.

They found that the Germans had fled, but six were captured later. It was an unique affair, and probably the first time in history that attacking troops had provided their own artillery fire. For his bravery and initiative, Sergeant Telling received the Commander in Chief's Certificate.

September 4th was another great day in the history of 30 Corps, for, driving forward from Alost, the 11th Armoured Division reached Antwerp, and received another tumultuous welcome. Armoured cars of the Inns of Court and tanks of the 3rd Royal Tank Regiment entered the city shortly after midday. Here again enemy resistance was only slight and very disorganised, and it was found that the Germans had not carried out any extensive demolitions in the harbour area. Mopping up continued throughout the day.

Next day, with the assistance of men of the Resistance Movement, Antwerp was finally cleared and about 3,000 prisoners taken. However, the tunnel under the Scheldt River was still held by the enemy, and they were in some strength on the North bank of the Albert Canal, over which all bridges had been blown as far East as Herenthals.

An example of luxurious O. P. work was given by an officer of the 64th Medium Regiment, who used to observe over the Canal from the top of a block of modern flats. To reach his post he entered a large lift each morning, and was whisked to the top, whence he crawled along the flat roof to his post.

Meanwhile, the 23rd Hussars had entered Mechelin, and, at one bridge which they captured, the Germans threw their guns into the river before surrendering. The Guards finally cleared up Brussels and the airfield at Evere, which had been occupied under shellfire the previous day by the 662nd Air O. P. Squadron.

By now, 20,000 prisoners had been taken by 30 Corps in their great advance. Club Route had been extended faster than ever before, some 250 miles having been covered in less than two weeks.

Although the enemy's defences had been thoroughly overrun and completely disorganised, it was obvious that he was going to make a stand on the line of the Albert Canal. However, the Boar's tail was up, and the enemy was given no time to consolidate, for, on September 6th, the Corps began to establish bridgeheads across the Canal.

The Guards made a rapid advance to the canal, despite the enthusiastic crowds along the route, who proved rather an embarrassment. At Beeringen, the Germans had replaced the old bridge, demolished earlier in the war, by a wooden structure. When the Welsh Guards arrived in the town they found this bridge partially demolished, and it was decided to cross by boat and assault the bridge from the Eastern side. Just before they were starting, however, a gallant patriot somehow managed to cross, and he reported that the Germans were pulling out. The Welsh Guards therefore made a precarious crossing and established a bridgehead, while the Sappers set to work to build another bridge alongside the demolished one.

North of Antwerp, the opposition had stiffened. The 4th Battalion, the King's Shropshire Light Infantry, forced a crossing of the river under heavy shelling and mortaring, and, during the whole of the day, our men were fiercely attacked by infantry and tanks. Accurate enemy shellfire prevented any bridging operations until late in the evening.

During the night of the 6th/7th September, the bridge at Beeringen was completed, in spite of the vicious shell and mortar fire from the enemy. The tanks of the 2nd (Armoured Recce) Welsh Guards crossed over in the early morning and passed Helchteren, after which they swung North towards Hechtel. Here strong opposition was met from German paratroops, but they were no match for the armour, and at least 500 were killed and 300 taken prisoner. Hechtel itself, however, was well held by troops with anti-tank guns and supported by a few SP guns, and the Guards were held up on the outskirts of the village.

Meanwhile, the battles North of Antwerp went on, and it was obvious that the enemy intended to deny us the use of the port as long as possible.

As the opposition stiffened, so it became necessary to get 30 Corps on to a narrower front. 12 Corps took over from the 11th Armoured Division in Antwerp, thus freeing the latter, which was then switched to the Beeringen bridgehead where the Guards were encountering fanatical opposition.

The 50th Division was now brought in on the left of the Guards, and, on September 8th, the 6th and 7th Battalions of the Green Howards established a small bridgehead over the Albert Canal just South of Gheel. The enemy was making frantic attempts to get at the Beeringen bridges and reduce the bridgehead, but in spite of the stubborn fighting no ground was lost. In the afternoon, two Regiments of the 8th Armoured Brigade crossed at Beeringen and pushed on to the support of the men of the 50th Division, who were now hard pressed. The armour met intense opposition in the area of the woods two miles northwest of Beeringen, and there was continued resistance and stern fighting all the way to Oosthan, which was reached that night. During the day, the two battalions of the 50th Division which had got over the Canal were called upon to repulse no less than four heavy counter-attacks. That day, also, the Royal Netherlands Brigade Group took over the immediate defence of the bridges at Beeringen from the Irish Guards.

Our men were now fighting in the 'Aldershot' of Belgium, with sand dunes, heather and fir trees everywhere. Bourg Leopold, the main barracks in the area, was still in enemy hands, and remained so until September 11th, when the 8th Armoured Brigade cleared the town.

The Welsh Guards continued to be heavily engaged in the area of the Hechtel crossroads. The parachuteless German parachutists were fighting with tremendous zeal, and were well supported by impressed men from the ground staffs of the Luftwaffe, who made up for their lack of military training by an abundance of fanatical bravery.

On the afternoon of September 8th, near the Hechtel crossroads, a report came through to the command post of the 2nd Welsh Guards that four enemy Panther tanks were threatening the position from the West. Lieutenant W. H. Griffiths volunteered to investigate the position, and went off in his tank. unaccompanied. He moved up the road from Hechtel to Bourg Leopold and was immediately fired at by a Panther, but the shell missed. Manoeuvring his tank into some woods South of the road, Lieutenant Griffiths waited until the Panther came to within fifty yards, and then he destroyed it in three shots. The three other Panthers were seen, but evidently deciding that discretion was needed, they moved away. Griffiths added to his bag by destroying two vehicles and then made his way back to the command post. His action undoubtedly broke up what might have been a serious threat to the left flank, and he was awarded the Military Cross.

During that night it became evident that the enemy had once again been reinforced, and it was estimated that there were no less than sixteen enemy battalions between the Escaut and the Albert Canals. Strong attacks were put in again on the men of the 50th Division, but these were all repulsed and bridging operations went on. An audacious attempt was made on the bridge at Beeringen when a suicide squad of one German officer and forty men made their way along the canal bank from the north-west. They succeeded in getting to within half a mile of the bridge and destroyed some thirty vehicles of the "A" Echelon of the 8th Armoured Brigade before being eliminated.

The most savage fighting took place at Hechtel, where the enemy still held on grimly. The crossroads there became a no-man's-land, with Hubner, a veteran of Alamein, and his battle group holding one side, and the Guards holding the other.

September 10th was another red-letter day for the Guards, for they made a dramatic dash for the Escaut Canal and succeeded in capturing what became known as "Joe's Bridge", a bridge at De Groot about ten miles North of Hechtel and only three miles from the Dutch frontier. It was decided that a surprise capture of the bridge outweighed in value the possible threat to our communications, but, to reach it, Hechtel would have to be by-passed, as it was still strongly held. Consequently, a troop of the Household Cavalry found a way round Hechtel to the West, along a rough track through the sand dunes, which rejoined the main road to the North about two miles above Hechtel. The Grenadier Group then fought its way North until it reached the level crossing a mile short of the bridge. Here it was held up by enemy fire from the fir woods on either side, and it was impossible for our tanks to deploy.

Meanwhile, the Irish Guards Group made good progress, and, as darkness fell, they reached the factory area southeast of the bridge. Major David Peel's squadron was instructed to rush the bridge as quickly as possible, and he moved up to the factory gates and debussed the infantry company which was under his command.

It was appreciated that any guns defending the bridge would be sited either at the Northern end of the bridge or at some cross-roads just South of it. Major Peel ordered Lieutenant D. Lampard's troop to patrol slowly forward towards the crossroads accompanied by an infantry platoon under the command of Lieutenant J. Stanley-Clarke, while the rest of the squadron gave covering fire.

The troops reached the crossroads, and the tanks took up positions among the houses on both sides of the road. They spotted an 88 mm gun being towed across the bridge and knocked it out. The infantry then moved up under covering fire, and, at a pre-arranged signal, the bridge was rushed by the tanks with the infantry doubling behind. Two of the tanks were disabled, and only Lieutenant Lampard's and Sergeant Steer's tanks reached the bridge. The six 88 mm guns guarding the bridge were knocked out, and a Royal Engineers officer, Lieutenant Hutton, dealt with the prepared demolition charges. The rest of the squadron then moved up, and the bridge was captured intact.

The speed of the advance and attack had taken the German gun crews completely by surprise, for it appeared that they had been expecting their own tanks, and not ours, and early in the proceedings the German gunners had abandoned their guns and made for a safer, if less heroic, position. It was learned that the sergeant in charge of the demolition squad had, earlier that day, made a stirring speech to the garrison in which he said, "The bridge must and will be blown, and every man will fight to the last round."

He had been, however, one of the first to leave the locality, forgetting, in his haste, to press the demolition switch.

On the left flank more counter-attacks were put in against our bridgehead over the Albert Canal, but these were all repulsed. That evening, the 6th Battalion, the Durham Light Infantry, got into Gheel, which they captured, together with 700 prisoners. On the right flank, the 11th Armoured Division, which had arrived from Antwerp, met with great success against two parachute battalions in the area of Helchteren, and some 200 of the enemy were wiped out while 450 more were captured.

The bridgehead over the Escaut Canal was extended the next day, and patrols crossed the Dutch border. During the day some SP guns approached the Irish Guards' positions southwest of the bridge. Major David Peel knocked out one of them, but, unfortunately, was killed while trying to locate another one. Hechtel, although by now surrounded, continued to hold out, and enemy troops were still in the woods to the North of Beeringen bridge.

The enemy's main attacks were against the bridgehead at Gheel, but these met with little success and cost the enemy dear. The position in Gheel was still rather confused, a thick fog combining with the smoke from the burning buildings helping to add to the general uncertainty. The enemy troops, too, were hopelessly lost, and had no idea where our troops were, or even where they were. It was learnt later that the enemy made an extraordinary penetration during the night with 400 infantry and 10 tanks, but only 50 men and 4 tanks got back. In their withdrawal, they ran into men of the Durhams, and some good shooting was had. One German tank commander put his head out of the turret within a hundred yards of a machine gun platoon, and stated in a loud voice:

"I want to die for Hitler!"

He did.

On the following day the bridgehead over the Escaut Canal was strengthened by the arrival of the 231st Infantry Brigade of the 50th Division, while the 11th Armoured Division cleared the ground up to the Canal on the Corps' right flank. 12 Corps took over the responsibility for the Gheel bridgehead to free the 50th Division for a further advance. At Hechtel, our troops withdrew during the night, and, soon after daybreak, a heavy concentration was put down on the village by Mediums and 4.2 Mortars. A determined attack was then put in by the 1st Welsh Guards, supported by the 2nd (Armoured Recce) Welsh Guards, and, after brisk fighting with SS troops, the village was finally cleared.

On September 13th, the Corps Commander paid a visit to men of the Guards Armoured Division and congratulated them on their successes, which he described as 'brilliant'.

During the next few days there was little enemy activity on the Corps front. The Germans evidently realised that our bridgehead over the Escaut Canal was now too strong for him to eliminate, and he transferred the full weight of his attacks onto the 12 Corps' bridgehead.

Once again the Resistance Movement activities had been excellent, and it was estimated, at this stage, that the Belgian Resistance Movement, since "D" Day, had been responsible for damage or destruction to the number of 976 locomotives and railway wagons. 80 trains had been derailed, and cuts made in over 1,000 railway lines and 300 telephone cables. In addition, successful attacks had been made on 29 railway bridges, 21 road bridges, and 11 lock gates.

The much-contested battle grounds of Belgium and Flanders had been over-run in record time, and swept clean of the enemy. The amazing advance of 30 Corps from the Seine had culminated in a firmly held bridgehead over the Escaut Canal, but there was to be no pause. The enemy was on the run, and he must be followed up without respite.

Ending a message to his troops, Field Marshal Sir Bernard Montgomery expressed the feelings of the fighting men:

"The triumphant cry now is — Forward into Germany! Good luck to you all. And, good hunting in Germany".

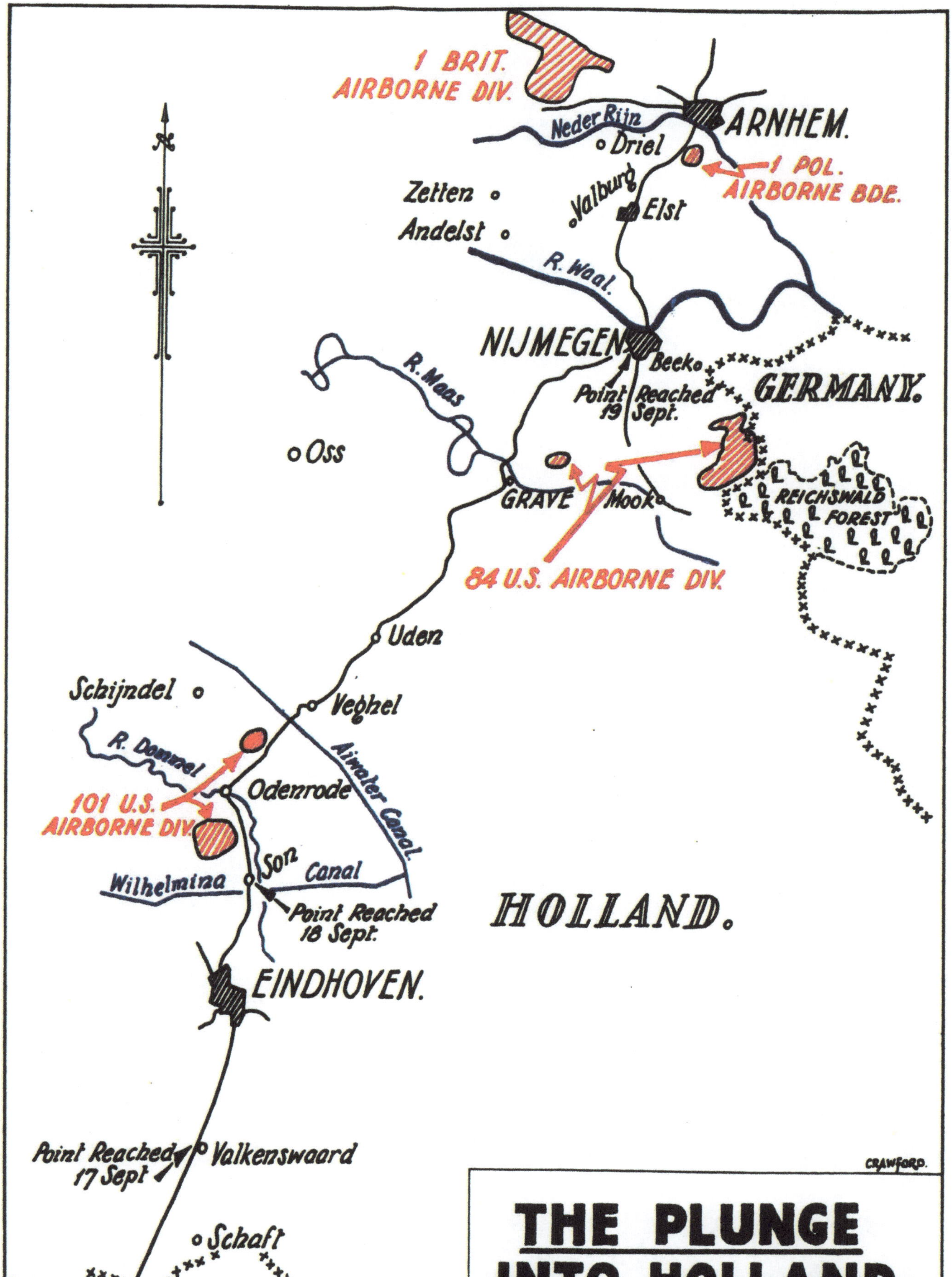
1 BRIT. AIRBORNE DIV.
Neder Rijn
ARNHEM.
Driel
1 POL. AIRBORNE BDE.
Zetten
Valburg
Elst
Andelst
R. Waal.
NIJMEGEN
Beek
GERMANY.
Point Reached 19 Sept.
R. Maas
Oss
GRAVE
Mook
REICHSWALD FOREST
84 U.S. AIRBORNE DIV.
Uden
Schijndel
Veghel
R. Dommel
Odenrode
Aiwater Canal
101 U.S. AIRBORNE DIV.
Son
Wilhelmina
Canal
Point Reached 18 Sept.
HOLLAND.
EINDHOVEN.
Point Reached 17 Sept
Valkenswaard
Schaft
BELGIUM.
CRAWFORD.
THE PLUNGE INTO HOLLAND
SCALE 1:400,000.
0
5
10
Miles

CHAPTER FIVE

THE PLUNGE INTO HOLLAND

For the next stage, the break-out from the bridgehead over the Escaut Canal, the 11th Armoured Division passed to the command of 8 Corps who had, meantime, arrived on our right flank. The 43rd Division now came up from the Seine area, where they had remained since the crossing of the river, and rejoined 30 Corps, so that we now had under command the Guards Armoured Division, the 43rd Division, and the 50th Division.

All the plans were made for another spectacular dash, this time Northwards into Holland, and it was hoped that this next operation would carry us right through to the Zuider Zee, thus allowing the Second Army to debouche into the North German Plain before winter set in, and cut off the Germans in Western Holland.

The Divisions of the Airborne Corps, the 1st British, the 82nd US, and the 101st US, were to be dropped simultaneously on September 17th to secure the crossings over the main Dutch waterways. The 101st was to take Eindhoven, and the water-crossings to the North; the 82nd was to capture the bridge at Grave over the River Maas, and the bridge at Nijmegen over the River Waal; and the 1st British was to seize the crossing of the Neder Rijn at Arnhem.

The Sappers' problems were many, and an enormous amount of bridging would be required. The detailed planning of the equipment needed, based on maps, air photos, local, verbal, and printed information, was done by a special planning team. Three Army Groups Royal Engineers were placed under command of the Corps for the operation. If all the bridges were demolished, it was estimated that no less than 2,277 vehicles would be required by the Royal Engineers.

The Guards' tanks were to make the break through from the bridgehead, and if they found that the bridges were blown, the next Division in the column, the 43rd, was to take over and assault the crossings while the Guards held the flanks.

On the right 8 Corps was to move up to protect the right flank, and on the left 12 Corps was to fulfil a similar task.

Soon after midday on the 17th, when he knew that the Airborne drop had been made, the Corps Commander gave the order to go. Difficult country lay ahead, marshy and heavily wooded, and full artillery and air support had been ordered. Consequently 300 guns of the Corps Artillery laid a rolling carpet of death along the axis, and seven squadrons of rocket-firing Typhoons roared ahead at five minute intervals to pounce upon and destroy anything German.

An RAF Squadron Leader was attached to the Irish Guards, and, although he was furious at having to fight the battle on the ground instead of in his Typhoon, he had entered into the plan with great enthusiasm, and knew almost by heart what each tank was to do.

Zero hour on the bridge over the Escaut was like the start of some improbable race, with the tanks lined up nose to tail waiting for the word to go. When the barrage began to move forward, the squadrons moved off, meeting only a little Spandau fire at first, but quite suddenly nine tanks were brewed up by 88 mm guns in the middle of the column. Many of the crews succeeded in baling out, but the only cover available was a number of slit trenches, many of them occupied by the enemy. One Guardsman plunged into a trench and found himself in the company of a fat and very frightened Hun, who at once made room for him, and offered him a large cigar. Another had a sharp scuffle with the German occupant of his trench, and shot him in the stomach. The wounded German fired back, and hit the Guardsman in the leg, but he quickly finished the Hun off.

After bitter fighting the leading tanks of the Irish Guards managed to enter Holland soon after three o'clock, but were held up again by enemy infantry entrenched beside the road and supported by SP guns. The Typhoons were called in, and with artillery support the road was cleared. On several occasions Typhoons engaged targets within 100 yards of our own tanks. The turning point in the battle came when Sergeant Cowan, commanding one of the Irish Guards' tanks, knocked out a German SP gun which was covering the road. The crew trotted in to surrender, and not only did they persuade the gun crew of another 88 — to surrender, but they willingly pointed out the positions occupied by their comrades.

The fighting became less grim, the advance became easier, and just before last light the Irish Guards Group reached the town of Valkenswaard where they bivouacked for the night. The effect of the Typhoon and tank attack on the Germans was to produce a complete breakdown of morale. They came in to surrender with tears running down their faces, and as the time could not be spared to deal with them, they were told to double back down the column. Many were still running in Olympic style when they reached Brigade HQ.

On the way through Valkensward an Intelligence Officer went to the Post Office, which also proved to be the German Town Major's HQ. The Town Major and his staff had disappeared, but the telephone was still working and while the Intelligence Officer was there, it rang. The caller was the German Commander at Eindhoven. He made an impassioned exhortation to the effect that Valkenswaard must be defended at all costs. Our officer fortunately knew German, and he replied that that was exactly what he intended to do.

The Engineers were called in at Valkenswaard to bridge an entirely unexpected gap over a stream and crater, and, in twelve hours, a 190 feet Class 40 Bailey Bridge was built.

At six o'clock the next morning the Guards, again led by the Irish Guards Group, continued their advance in the face of determined opposition. The enemy was using Panther tanks, and their infantry was making full use of the wooded country which lined each side of the road. However progress was made, and by the evening the Irish Guards had linked up with the 101st US Airborne Division at Eindhoven.

Eindhoven is a typical Dutch town, clean and fresh, and had not been greatly damaged. The huge Phillips Radio Factory is its main feature and its main industry, and although it had been a target for the RAF, a small part of it had been able to keep up production. Under the German occupation the Dutch staff had been forced to produce wireless components. Supervision was strict, and the chances of sabotage slight. However, at just one stage there was no supervision. This was after the boxes had been packed on the top floor before loading on to the guarded lorries. The Germans evidently thought there was no need for supervision here, but the wily Dutchman always saw that the boxes containing the delicate parts made their own way downstairs, aided by a good stout pair of Dutch boots.

The populace gave a great welcome first to the US Airborne boys, and then to our own lads as they rolled in. None, however, received a more rapturous welcome than some members of the Netherlands Brigade, who took part in this operation, and were the first Dutch troops that the good people of Eindhoven had seen since the occupation.

One of our columns was standing in the main street. Soldiers, surrounded by the excited populace, were giving away cigarettes right and left, and receiving kisses and fruit in exchange. Suddenly, riding slowly past the column, came a despatch rider. He attracted little attention at first, until some Dutch women spotted his shoulder flash — the Netherlands flash! A real Dutch soldier! The British column and the British soldiers were immediately forgotten. The Netherlands representative disappeared from sight under a pile of raving women, and the crowd moved off up the street with their soldier still submerged. Dutchmen fought for the privilege of wheeling his motor-cycle. . . . .

Half an hour later he rolled into view again, full of Bols gin, and kissed into a state of blissful coma. With difficulty he mounted his motor-cycle, received a last kiss for luck from everybody, and wobbled off up the road. He fell off after ten yards, but willing hands helped him on again, and finally, with three children on his pillion, and bunches of orange flowers tied all over him and his machine, he zig-zagged out of sight.

Unfortunately the new-found happiness of the inhabitants was marred by the vicious air-raid the Germans staged the night after the liberation. Considerable material damage was done, and there were many casualties. Our transport, jammed in the town, presented an easy target, and there were most spectacular firework displays as ammunition trucks caught fire.

At this stage of the battle the 50th Division passed temporarily to the operational command of 8 Corps, as it was decided that 30 Corps should be relieved of the responsibility of safeguarding their axis from the bridgehead to Eindhoven.

Meanwhile the flanks had had stiff fighting, but 8 Corps had now a small bridgehead over the Meuse — Escaut Canal in the area Lille — St Hubert, and 12 Corps, on the left flank, had established another bridgehead over the same canal, with two Brigades across on the Northern banks.

The bridge across the Wilhelmina Canal on the main axis at Son was blown, but during the night the Engineers, aided by German prisoners, worked like demons, and at first light the 5th Guards Brigade were able to cross a Class 40 bridge, which had been built in ten hours, and race forward to Grave and Nijmegen.

It was a cold morning, but the tank crews were elated by the chase, and pressed on eagerly. The bridges along the route were held by American Airborne men who cheered the British tanks as they roared by. The Americans, who had had previous experience in Normandy, and earlier in the Mediterranean Campaign, had done a fine job. They had taken the great bridge across the Maas at Grave without a fight. This was certainly an unexpected pleasure, for if the Germans had succeeded in demolishing this nine-span bridge, valuable time would have been lost, and the Engineers would have had to undertake a major bridging operation. The bridge had been damaged by shelling and bombing, and the roadway was holed in several places. Consequently it was fit for one-way traffic only, but, in three days, a Field Company of Army Troops RE repaired it up to Class 70 standard.

As they approached the bridge the leading tanks were met by Lieut General FAM Browning, the Airborne Corps Commander, and he conferred with the Battalion Commanders and the Brigadier. It was a particularly happy meeting as one of the leading Battalions had been commanded by Lieut General Browning six years before.

Meanwhile our flanking Corps, still meeting strong opposition, had been unable to keep pace with us, and we were very much on our own. The enemy, although disconcerted, had still sufficient forces close enough to the rapidly extending route to threaten it.

Even as far back as Schaft, a little village only just a mile from Club Route, and just beyond the Belgian border, there was still fighting. The 90th City of London Field Regiment RA, travelling along the main axis, ordered one of their batteries to deploy to the right of Club Route, a few hundred yards from Schaft. The gun position proved to be ahead of the leading infantry, a Battalion of the Devons, who were halted outside the village, making their plans for attack. Battery Sergeant Major Wilson on a motor-cycle, with L/Sergeant Krelle riding pillion, went forward to recce positions for forward defence posts. In the village civilians warned them that the Germans were in the vicinity, and they also told them that there was a wounded Tommy in a house at the far end of the village. They found a Major of the Divisional Anti-tank Regiment, badly wounded, and after examination, they decided that it would be dangerous to move him.

They set off at a good pace to return to the battery and report the situation, but had not gone very far when a German with a nasty line in light automatics stepped out of the hedge and gave them a burst at close range. Wilson swerved the bike to the other side, and the two men dived for the ditch without delay. A further party of trigger-pulling Germans arrived, and it looked to Wilson and his friend as if they were well and truly "in the bag". However, Krelle made a run for it, and Wilson followed suit. In fact he passed Krelle very quickly. For about 150 yards across a stubble field, with bullets zipping around them, they kept up a fine turn of speed, clearing a wide ditch in their stride, and finally reached cover among some school buildings, whence they were able to get back to their battery.

The Medical Officer was advised, and after some discussion, it was decided that the MO himself, Captain Lloyd, accompanied by Driver Kessler and a Sergeant would try to get into the village. With their Red Cross flying, they reached the house without interference. Here they found a German who could speak French, and after some discussion the Doctor was allowed to attend to the wounded Major. A German Officer now appeared, and the MO told him that he intended to take the wounded Major back with him. The Hun agreed to this on the condition that a German Officer was returned from a Prisoner of War Cage in his place.

Kessler and the Sergeant were ordered to return in the Jeep and collect a German Officer, while the MO was held as a hostage. Off they went, and eventually had to go as far back as Bourg Leopold in Belgium before the necessary prisoner could be obtained. The mass of double-banking traffic coming up Club Route made their progress slow, but late in the afternoon they got back to the village with their prisoner, The attack was delayed while the exchange was made, although the Germans would not allow the party to return until after dark. Regrettably the Major died.

Meanwhile, further North, the Guards had linked up with the 82nd US Airborne Division, and had cleared up to the town of Nijmegen South of the river.

The Americans had found the situation in Nijmegen more difficult than had been anticipated, and they had not managed to capture the massive bridge across the Waal, so essential to our successful advance, and which was known to be prepared for demolition. It was covered from the North side by a considerable Hun force, Germans were positioned among the girders of the bridge, and others were expectantly waiting at the demolition switches for the order to blow. The position was not too promising. To clear the bridge a combined Guards and Airborne attack was put in, but this failed.

The next day, however, an American Regimental Combat Team undertook a daylight assault crossing to the West of the bridge. General Gavin, commander of the 82nd US Airborne Division made this Combat Team ready at once, although his Division was being counter attacked South East of Nijmegen, and could ill afford to spare any men.

The tanks of the Irish Guards worked steadily forward during the morning, clearing the Germans out of isolated positions in the Western outskirts of Nijmegen, South of the Waal, and it was not until two o'clock in the afternoon that the Americans could get down to the river bank at the place chosen for the crossing.

Then, a combined plan had to be made, as the Americans were to use British assault boats, lent to them by the Guards Armoured Division for the crossing, and they were to be supported by the fire of both British and American Artillery, plus the Irish Guards' tanks firing from behind the river bank.

The difficulties were enormous, for the Waal is broad and swift running. Further, it was daylight, the Germans were in force on the far bank, and the Americans had had no previous experience of our assault boats. Yet the leading wave started to cross at three o'clock, only one hour after their arrival.

The gallant Americans rushed the defences on the far bank and established a small, precarious bridgehead. After stiff fighting, they captured a strongly defended dyke bank and came upon the defenders of the bridge from behind. By six o'clock the American flag was seen to be flying on the Northern end of the railway bridge.

This magnificent assault is probably one of the most amazing achievements of the war, and it could have been carried out only by a very fine Division.

A squadron of the Grenadier Guards was now ordered to get across the road bridge at all costs, and link up with the Americans. No 1 Troop was given the task of leading the way, and the acting Troop Leader, Sergeant P Robinson, moved towards the first span. His tank was hit by an 88 mm, and the wireless was put out of action. He pulled back behind a bank, and changed tanks with L/Sergeant Billingham in order to maintain wireless communication with his Squadron Leader. At the same time L/Sergeant Pacey moved his tank up alongside, and destroyed the 88 mm gun with a few rounds. By this time a number of 88 mm and automatic weapons were engaging the troop, but the order was to push on, so Sergeant Pacey led the way on to the bridge. On the bridge, Sergeant Robinson could see anti-tank guns firing at them from the other side, and they had not travelled 50 yards when a panzerfaust hit a girder above them. Projectiles seemed to come from every angle but the tanks were not hit. Snipers in the girders dropped grenades, and fired at the tanks in an effort to make them close down, but they reached the far side, only to find the road obstructed by a block. By swinging their tanks broadside they managed to break through this, and Sergeant Robinson once more took the lead. Firing their guns as they went the troop pushed on towards the railway bridge, where they joined up with the American paratroopers.

Two of the tanks of this troop were hit by panzerfausts after crossing the bridge, but Sergeant Robinson and the other tank took up a position astride the main road to Arnhem. Captain the Lord Carrington arrived on the scene, and sent an American patrol back to the bridge, where they found one of the tanks which had been hit, guarded by its driver, Sergeant Knight MM. The rest of the crew had been taken prisoner, but the tank was still a runner, and so the crew was made up by two Americans. Other troops crossed, and the bridgehead was held under shellfire all that night until the Irish Guards took it over the next day.

When it is remenbered that the Nijmegen Bridge is approximately 400 yards long, with an embankment of equal length on the far side, which prevented deployment of tanks, it can be appreciated that this dash was no picnic. An RE officer, following the tanks on foot found that charges had been laid under the second span, and they were quite sufficient to destroy it. During his task of removing the charges he captured over 70 prisoners from the roomes which had been built into the buttresses. It will remain a mystery why this important bridge was not destroyed, and although many reasons have been given for its preservation, the real reason has never been discovered.

On the same day the Germans made their first attempt to cut Club Route. This was in the vicinity of Son — St Odenrode, and although Corps traffic was held up for three important hours, the attack was finally repulsed, and Club Route was still intact..

Meanwhile there was little news of the 1st Airborne Division which had been dropped at Arnhem on September 17th as planned. It was known that the bridge at Arnhem, over the Neder Rijn, was intact, but it was not known whether it was in our hands or not. However, on the 21st a station with a strange code-sign was heard on the Regimental net of the 64th Medium Regiment RA, urgently calling for artillery support. When asked who it was calling, the voice replied: "The people you are trying to join up with." This could only mean the 1st Airborne Division. After further checking, it was finally established that the caller was the CRA of this Division, and from that moment invaluable artillery support was given to the hard pressed Airborne troops.

How invaluable that support proved to be, and how much it was appreciated is shown in the following message received by the 64th Medium Regiment from the Commander of the 1st Airborne Division, in which the Regiment was granted the privilege of wearing the Airborne flash.

> "On behalf of the 1st Airborne Division, I wish to thank you, your Regiment and 419 Heavy Battery, for the support given to us during the past week.
>
> It is quite obvious now that the part the Regiment played in the Battle of Arnhem was a deciding factor in the survival

THE GUARDS ARMOURED DIVISION RUMBLE ACROSS THE NIJMEGEN BRIDGE IMMEDIATELY AFTER THEY HAD CAPTURED IT

of the Division for the nine days it spent North of the River Rhine. At the time your Regiment came into action in support of us, things were looking fairly black and your fire just made all the difference. It was not only the devastating and very accurate effect produced by your fire during the last six days of our battle that had such a heartening effect on all ranks of the Division, but also the way in which all calls were so promptly answered.

The Commander of 30 Corps and the Airborne Corps have agreed to our request that we may be allowed to present your Regiment with our Airborne sign, the Pegasus, to be worn on the lower half of the right sleeve. We shall regard it as a great privilege if you will undertake to wear this as a lasting remembrance of our liaison during the Battle of Arnhem.

Signed RL Urquhart
Major General.

On the morning of the 21st the Guards were ordered to advance as fast as possible in order to link up with the Airborne Division. But the road forward was merely a causeway through low-lying, marshy fields, and it was impossible for tanks to deploy off the roads.

In addition, the weather had broken, and conditions were appalling for the remainder of the operation. It was obvious that the situation called for infantry, and the whole of the 43rd Division, which was now arriving at Nijmegen, was ordered forward to press the attack.

In Nijmegen itself mopping up of isolated pockets of Germans was still going on with the enthusiastic, but slightly embarrassing assistance of the civilian population. Captain Andrew of the 5th Battalion, the Dorset Regiment, was engaged in this task, when shots came from a warehouse some 100 yards in front of him. He immediately ordered a section to get around behind the warehouse and deal with the situation, while a machine gun gave covering fire from the front. He took up his position behind a tree, and watched anxiously. It was a tense moment.

At this point he felt a touch on his shoulder, and whipped round, revolver at the ready, to find himself facing a charming Dutch lady, who, in excellent English, asked him if he would be good enough to accept the pot of jam she had brought for him.

"Oh! thanks!" he said, thoroughly flabbergasted. As she walked calmly away Captain Andrew glanced back at the warehouse in time to see three Germans being escorted from it.

"Well I'll be damned!" he thought, "What hospitality! What a war!"

The following day, September 22nd, the 43rd Division began

to push forward encountering very stiff opposition. Little progress could be made until the evening, when a mobile column of the 5th Battalion, the Duke of Cornwall's Light Infantry, mounted on the tanks of the 4th/7th Dragoon Guards, carrying with them supplies in Dukws, broke through and made their way by side roads to the Southern bank of the Neder Rijn. They made contact with Polish parachutists who had been dropped at Driel, an advance of nearly 10 miles in under 30 minutes.

During this dash there was considerable opposition and confusion. CSM Philp, DCM, in the rear vehicle of the column during this advance noticed something peculiar going on behind. He quickly realized what was happening, and turning to his driver said: "Don't look now, but we're being followed by Tigers." And this was indeed the case, the Tiger tanks, all unaware that they had got into an enemy column, were following up at the correct road spacing. The news was passed forward, and an ambush was arranged farther up the column. In due course the Tigers ran into the trap, the leader was knocked out, the second one ran into him, and the remainder ditched themselves in their panic. The Commanding Officer of the 5th DCLI, Lieut Colonel G Taylor, was awarded a bar to his DSO for his part in the Battalion's brilliant break through to the banks of the Neder Rijn.

Also on the 22nd, patrols of the Household Cavalry Regiment (armoured cars) were operating on the South bank of the Neder Rijn. They sighted a steamer towing four barges, and shortly afterwards reported that they had damaged the steamer, and sunk three barges. They received back the message: "Congratulations on brilliant naval action. Splice the mainbrace." It is understood that they did so.

Further over to the left the 43rd Reconnaissance Regiment was holding the flank. One squadron rolled into Andelst, where they were rapturously greeted by the joyful population in spite of their unshaven chins and drenched appearance. Amongst those who greeted them was the complete crew of a Dakota, who had been hiding in the village since their plane had been forced down during the Arnhem drop. From the station of Andelst-Zetten it was found possible to ring down the line to the station master of the next station, which was in German hands. He gave them a good deal of information, including the important fact that the Germans were rushing up reinforcements in front of their position.

On the right flank, to meet the danger of a possible German counter thrust from the Reichswald Forest, the Coldstream Guards were placed under the command of the 82nd Airborne Division.

On the night of the 23rd an attempt was made to get supplies across the river to the Airborne troops but this failed owing to the steepness of the banks and the intense fire the Germans were putting down. However, as the weather cleared a little, long lines of Stirlings flew in at zero feet to make sure of dropping their supplies in the right places. The bravery of these pilots was magnificent, for the flak was intense and losses high.

Meanwhile along the Arnhem road the advance was going slowly owing to very stiff opposition, and the infantry were held up South of Elst.

B Company of the 5th Battalion, the Wiltshire Regiment, advanced along the railway line until they came under intense fire and had to dig in around a signal box. Movement by daylight was impossible and this little band of men remained virtually cut off from the Battalion for three days. For food they used chickens they found in the garden of the signal box, and for cigarettes they rolled dried leaves in paper.

They found a goat, and tied a red signal flag round its middle, a green one round its hindquarters, stuck an apple on each of its horns, and painted its tail with tar. Then they gave it a spank, and sent it trotting off to join the astonished Germans, whose positions were less than 50 yards away.

It was on September 22nd that the enemy succeeded in cutting Club Route for the first time. Using tanks and lorried infantry, he attacked from the North West, and cut the route between Uden and Veghel. To restore the situation, the Corps Commander ordered the 32nd Guards Brigade to move back with all speed from Nijmegen. That night the route remained breached, and vital supplies were held up for 25 important hours.

When the route was cut the Corps Commander was meeting the Army Commander at Veghel, and that evening he found himself cut off from his Tactical HQ. He had to get back to make vital decisions, and a battalion of the Durham Light Infantry said that they knew a way round the breach, but that the route could only be traversed by Bren carriers. The next morning the General set off with an escort of six carriers, and succeeded in evading the Germans and reaching his HQ.

The day produced a remarkable number of senior officers stranded in the forward areas after having been shot down in Auster aircraft over the axis. They included the Chief of Staff Second Army, the Brigadier of the Royal Artillery, and a senior Air Officer from Transport Command.

Next day a combined British and American effort was made from the South to break the enemy's grip on the route, and despite uncomfortably accurate shellfire, they had, by the afternoon, been able to link up with tanks of the Irish Guards which had dashed down from the North.

Club Route was free again, and badly needed supplies could move forward without hindrance. But not for long; for on the night of the 24th/25th of September elements of the German 6th Parachute Regiment made a determined attack South of Veghel, and succeeded in cutting our main artery again.

Caught by the hail of shellfire, drivers of vehicles were forced to take cover in the ditches. Brigadier H L Glyn Hughes DSO MC, of 8 Corps, who was visiting the 30 Corps area at the time, organised the drivers, who were armed with rifles, into a local defence body. With this force he held off the enemy until some tanks arrived. The Brigadier briefed the tank commanders, and then encouraged the drivers to return to their vehicles and drive them to safety. He stood in the open road, until an enemy SP gun approached to within 80 yards of him. For this action Brigadier Glyn Hughes was awarded a second bar to his DSO.

Also at the time of the breach, two squadrons of the 52nd (Lowland) Reconnaissance Regiment were moving up to Veghel from St Odenrode when they ran into heavy shellfire. The Corps Commander, who was in the vicinity, put the two squadrons under the command of the 101st US Airborne Division. As it was getting dark the American Commander decided that no effective measures could be taken that evening to restore the line of communications. However the following morning a combined attack was made, which went well for about 600 yards, and then began to get sticky and eventually stopped. There was incessant enemy shell and mortar fire, and the closeness of the country was made full use of by enemy snipers. Later in the day more infantry were put into the attack, and with the Guards moving down from the North, the enemy was forced to withdraw.

As was only to be expected the enemy's efforts resulted in the capture of a number of vehicles and men. One man, Driver G Ferguson, of 536 Company RASC, which was moving up to Nijmegen at the time, managed to elude his captors, and spent three days and nights in the loft of a house where the enemy set up a HQ. Indeed, one night Driver Ferguson had the company of some German soldiers in the same loft, but managed to hide himself by burrowing into a pile of wheat sacks. During these three days and nights he had nothing to eat or drink, and he gave a hearty welcome to the Americans who rescued him.

Meanwhile very heavy fighting had been taking place (September 23rd and 24th) on the Arnhem road, where elements of the Guards and the 43rd Division were still engaged. They were now reinforced by the leading brigade of the 50th Division under command of the Corps again, but little progress was made.

The Guards Armoured Divisional HQ troop of tanks, and the defence platoon had a purely protective role, but they were always eager for a fight. They had been sent to investigate the village of Oss, a few miles West of Club Route, and in no man's land. They found a large number of Germans there, and this Lilliputian force attacked them so ferociously that they routed the enemy and returned in triumph with 80 prisoners, having killed and wounded many others.

About this time supplies were getting low, but the Germans had providentially amassed a huge dump of food at Oss. Its guardian was an ancient Dutchman, appointed by the Germans, and as he seemed an agreeable and capable custodian it was not thought necessary to furnish any further guard. He was a pleasant old man, only too willing to issue the supplies to anyone who was willing to sign for them. For a day or two everything went smoothly, the Quartermasters drawing their needs, and signing with pleasure. But it came as a shock to one Quartermaster, who, as he was signing, noticed that the signature previous to his own was that of a German Army Captain. The ancient custodian cheerfully agreed that this was correct, and thereafter his staff was increased by a party of Tommies.

The whole of this time Nijmegen was under shellfire. The main bridge had come in for a considerable amount of attention both from enemy artillery and aircraft, but had suffered very little damage. By night Nijmegen was well and truly lit up by many fires started by the indiscriminate shelling.

It now became apparent that the gallant 1st Airborne Division was in a very precarious state. The small area of country they occupied was completely overlooked, and Arnhem was firmly held by the enemy. Casualties had been very high, and there was a shortage of supplies, which, in any case, could only be provided by night on a limited scale. Each night, with the support of the whole of the Corps Artillery, efforts were made to reinforce and get supplies into the limited bridgehead held by the Airborne Division. Large numbers of assault boats were lost nightly, and lack of these essential craft precluded any large scale river crossing operation. 30 Corps artillery and a constant procession of Typhoons was all the support that could be given to them — and it was not enough. And so the order for the withdrawal of the Airborne garrison was given.

Owing to the full enemy observation any rescue bid had to be made by night. The operation began disastrously as the first assault boats fell into enemy hands on the way to the embarkation point, and replacements arrived only just in time for the attempt.

On the night of September 24th the 4th Battalion, the Dorset Regiment, prepared to make a crossing of the Neder Rijn. Supported by a heavy artillery barrage, the men launched their boats with difficulty and with "A" Company in the lead, made their way across the river. By now the enemy was getting anxious, and opened up with heavy machine gun fire on fixed lines across the river. It was a gallant crossing, casualties were high, and only 350 men got across. A small bridgehead was established, and during the following day the Dorsets fought their way in small parties to the only high ground in the vicinity, and held on to this in spite of the repeated efforts of the Germans to dislodge them.

One anti-tank gun crew was dug in about 60 yards from the river. They were under continual fire from close range, and some Germans got near enough to roll grenades down on to them. The Germans called on them to surrender, but Lance Corporal Stradling answered for all the men in no uncertain manner.

The evacuation of the exhausted Airborne men was planned for the night of the 25th/26th of September. The Dorsets were to cover the withdrawal. As part of the plan a feint assault crossing was staged downstream. A heavy artillery barrage was fired, and mobile machine gunners engaged the enemy from the Southern bank. During this operation, field guns of the Corps began to get dangerously short of ammunition — one regiment being down to five rounds per gun. Approximately 2,200 men of the Airborne Division were successfully evacuated, but the cost to the Dorset Battalion was high, and some 170 men failed to return.

The Sappers who were manning the boats which were bringing the Airborne troops back suffered so many casualties that volunteers were called for to help operate the boats. Men of the 5th Battalion, the Dorset Regiment gladly came forward. Their unusual task was rendered more difficult by the strong current and high wind. However, they did the job well, and one party even brought back a German who had got mixed up with the Airborne queue in the darkness. His delight on reaching the safety of the British lines was immense.

Some of the stout-hearted Airborne boys, too impatient to get back to await their turn in the boats, decided to swim across. They destroyed their equipment, and discarded most of their clothing, and consequently arrived on the friendly side distinctly underclad. They collected what they could — blankets, rags, sacking, or articles of women's clothing, and thus magnificently attired, laughed and joked in the greatest of spirits, and made short work of the many mugs of tea that were on offer.

The Q organisation of the 43rd Division had made excellent arrangements (under the circumstances) for their reception. A large barn had been fitted up as a reception centre, and signs pointed the way to it from the river bank. The lighting arrangements were simple — a Jeep was driven inside, and its headlights provided the illumination.

Blankets, rum, tea, and stew, were all constantly available, and although the resources were strained the supplies held out, and were much appreciated.

One small Cockney was asked how he felt.

"Awlright mate!" he said cheerfully, "Cor blimey! If only my mother could see me now!"

He was certainly a sight for the gods, with a coat and a pair of trousers far, far too large for him, and he was bare-footed, but he was completely happy.

Another inspiring sight was a Major who had swum the river fully dressed, even carrying his pistol. He refused all offers of tea, and marched away up the road as stiff and straight as if he had been on the barrack square.

Dukws transported the weary Airborne men back to Nijmegen. Even this was a perilous journey owing to the appalling weather conditions and the narrowness of the muddy, dyke-flanked roads.

Owing to the steeepness of the banks of the Neder Rijn the Dukws had not been able to give their usual help in the evacuation. In fact, when the Dorsets had put in their assault crossing six Dukws had been standing by to ferry across important supplies. Of these six only three were able to get into the water, and everyone of these stuck in the mud on the other side. All efforts to free them were useless, and eventually Corporal Varney and Driver Chilton swam back for help. For their bravery and coolness both these men were awarded the MM.

With the evacuation of the Airborne troops came the end of our great attempt to outflank the Reich in one bound. Two of the three great rivers had been crossed, and the Second Army had obtained a firm hold on German occupied Holland.

Much has been written about the gallant enterprise of the Airborne men, which resulted in so great a depletion of their numbers, but the loss was not in vain, for during the vital period they had successfully held off a large enemy force which would otherwise have beeen used to prevent the capture of the Nijmegen bridge.

30 Corps had made every effort to link up with the Airborne Division, but it had been difficult country for tanks, and the enemy troops had been skilfully handled to cause the maximum delay to our advance, an easy task in the canalised countryside.

It might just have been possible had not the Corps' lines of communication been continuously interfered with. When the Germans cut the axis they prevented the arrival of ammunition and the vital assault boats. Food, too, was beginning to get short, although this did not actually impede the operation. It was the first time that Club Route had been cut. The breaks had been quickly repaired, and, in a period of ten days, in spite of everything that the enemy could do, Club Route had been extended over sixty miles, and more than 25,000 vehicles had passed up this famous axis.

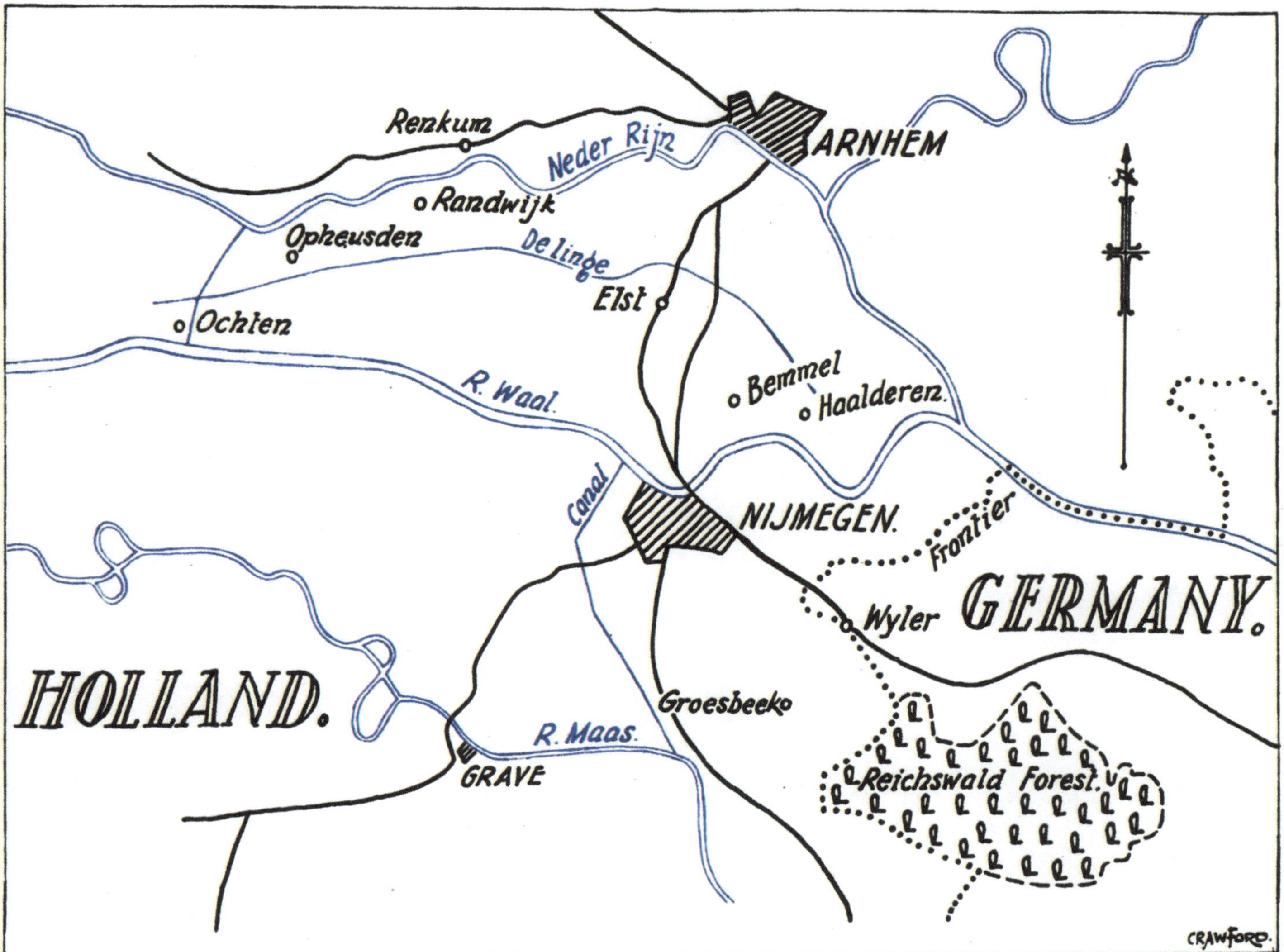

ISLAND INTERLUDE.

SCALE 1:200,000.

0 1 2 3 4 5 6 7 8 9 10

• Miles •

CHAPTER SIX

ISLAND INTERLUDE

Between the Waal and the Neder Rijn lies a large expanse of unattractive country known as the "Island". It is quite truthfully an Island, bounded as it is on the flanks by canals joining the two great rivers. It is flat, marshy, country containing some large villages and scattered farmsteads, but these were quickly reduced to ruins during the operations, and the "Island" became a very desolate spot. Those of our troops who were unfortunate enough to garrison the area will long remember the horrible weather conditions. In addition, from the time the Airborne Division was evacuated from Arnhem until the Corps moved South in early November, there was constant harassing fighting on the "Island", and the enemy launched several heavy attacks in an effort to regain control of the Nijmegen bridge.

From some factory buildings on the Northern bank of the Waal about three miles up-stream from the town, the Hun had observation of the road bridge. The railway bridge, which also carried road traffic, lies some distance to the West of the road bridge. From September 26th, for three days, he made every effort to destroy the two bridges, using artillery and large numbers of fighter-bombers. The attacks did a little damage to both bridges, but they remained open to traffic.

Having failed in his attempts the enemy resorted to other methods. In the early hours of the morning of September 29th he sent his Frogmen down the river from the East. These men were Naval personnel, who had been trained at Venice in long distance swimming under water with special equipment. They wore tight fitting rubber suits and breathing masks. Their feet had large flappers attached to them, and the only weapon that they carried was a sheath knife. They were complete even to waterproof wrist-watches.

They swam down the Waal that cold morning towing two large, torpedo-like explosive charges which were destined to be fastened to the road bridge and the railway bridge. They were so designed that when they were placed in a vertical position the time mechanism came into action, and, after allowing the swimmers time to get clear, they exploded.

The Frogmen had no difficulty in swimming under the wire boom which had been positioned across the river, but the current gave them some trouble when they reached the bridges, and they found they could not fasten the charges in a vertical position. They were placed horizontally, and emergency igniters were used. The charge fastened to the road bridge failed, although part of it exploded and caused superficial damage. The attack on the railway bridge was more successful, and as a result of the explosion one span collapsed.

The swimmers made good their escape, swimming on down the river in a Westerly direction, and intending to land in the German positions around Ochten. They landed too early however, and were all captured, with the exception of two, who were never accounted for, and are believed to have been killed.

One party landed in front of a 43rd Reconnaissance Regiment patrol, commanded by Sergeant W Ward. The patrol promptly opened fire on them with a Bren gun. One young sailor surrendered at once, the others swam across the river, where they were picked up by a party of Dutch Resistance men, and returned to the Recce patrol by boat. They were tough, and surly, but they were obviously very fit men, and had a great deal of courage.

The partial success of this unusual attempt to destroy the bridges led to unusual measures being taken for protection against a second effort. Every night a Dukw was employed patrolling the river between the two bridges with headlights blazing. The bridges themselves were floodlit by powerful searchlights, and Anti-tank gunners dug in their guns on the bank, and waited hopefully for anything that might come down the river. Floating logs came in for a good deal of attention, and this proved an unpopular sport with the troops on the other side as, on many occasions, the bullets ricochetted off the water. The possibility of an attack by one-man submarines was not overlooked, but for some reason or other the Hun never tried this method.

The 43rd Division and the 50th Division were still holding the "Island" bridgehead. A squadron of the 43rd Reconnaissance Regiment were holding positions on the Southern bank of the Neder Rijn at Randwijk when, on the 27th of September, about 350 fanatical Huns slipped across the river in the grey light of dawn, and launched a fierce attack against the thinly held observation positions. After inflicting some casualties, the Recce men were forced to withdraw. One armoured car was cut off from the squadron, and in an effort to avoid capture, fell from the narrow road into the steep dyke. The crew were captured.

The following day the Squadron returned, reinforced by the tanks of the 8th Armoured Brigade, and drove the Boche back into the river with heavy casualties.

Meanwhile a series of attacks were launched against our positions to the South East of Nijmegen, the strongest coming from the direction of Wyler. The enemy gained possession of some woods just South of Wyler, but lost five out of twelve tanks in doing so. On all parts of the Corps front the enemy seemed to be trying to build up his forces, and seize jumping off places for his assault on the bridges. It is now known that Hitler personally ordered the elimination of our bridge-head over the Waal.

By the 1st of October the enemy had gathered together a sizeable armoured force, and he made several determined attacks South from Arnhem towards Nijmegen, but after hard fighting the infantry, who were well prepared, managed to hold all the attacks.

A Battalion of the Green Howards under command of 50th Division were warned of the impending attack by the rumbling of enemy tanks in front of their positions at Bemmel, and by increased shelling and mortaring. This Battalion, the 7th, was under command of Major WFB Lloyd, his commanding officer having been wounded the previous day. The Battalion stood to, and in the early light of dawn, infantry, supported by tanks, attacked the forward companies. Communications with these companies were unsatisfactory, and Major Lloyd made several visits during the day to the forward positions in order to keep in touch with the situation.

The intense mortaring and shelling continued almost without a break, and during the morning and afternoon the enemy made further determined attacks with his infantry and tanks. At one part of the afternoon one company and two platoons of another were over-run. By moving up part of a carrier platoon the Major re-organised the position. The position became more serious when Spandau teams worked their way round behind. Fortunately, at this point, a troop of tanks arrived, and Major Lloyd led them personally against the enemy, and wiped them out.

As a result of this action the Battalion killed a large number of Germans and destroyed eight tanks. Moreover all its positions were handed over intact to the unit which relieved them late that night. Major Lloyd's energy, resource, and complete disregard for his own safety won for him the Distinguished Service Order.

During that night the enemy shifted the weight of his attack from the "Island" to the front South East of Nijmegen, but, if any ground was lost by us, it was quickly regained by a counter attack, and the enemy suffered heavy losses.

It was obvious that the enemy divisions were being strained to the utmost. The American attack had gone in further South in the direction of Aachen, and was giving the Germans plenty to think about. In addition our flanking Corps were pushing forward, and large parties of the enemy were still locked up in the Channel Ports. Although our old opponents, the 9th and 116th Panzer Divisions, were identified on the Corps front, not all the troops encountered at this period were of the same quality. The Hun was calling in all sorts and conditions of men to bolster up his strength. He had, for instance, a "Stomach Battalion", consisting, except for the higher ranks, of gentlemen suffering from stomach complaints.

He had, too, an "Eye Battalion" for those with some optical weakness. One man of this Battalion, when captured, was found to have the following exemption order: "Gefreiter Hans Muller is blind in his left eye, and the vision of the right eye is seriously diminished. He is unable to recognise a superior in the street, and therefore medically exempt from saluting."

Such consideration on the part of the Germans was not only extended to their own troops, but also to their enemies, as the following captured German order shows: "It is forbidden to tie Russians to the field kitchens during movement."

There was also the "Ear Battalion" for men who were hard of hearing. Some of the men were actually completely deaf. A Company Sergeant Major from this Battalion, who was captured, volunteered the information that Platoon Commanders were too scared to inspect the guards, because, as they could not hear anyone approach, they pulled the trigger automatically whenever anyone suddenly appeared. Two Sergeants of the guard had already been killed in this way.

At this stage of the war it was estimated that sixty-five per-cent of the prisoners taken were glad to be captured, although some would not admit it. There was for example the magnificent statement made by an officer who was captured about this time: "Do not get the impression that I am a coward because I have let myself become a prisoner. I would gladly have died a hero's death, but I thought it only fair and just to share the misfortunes of my men."

Those who were glad to be captured were usually either boys, or men over 30. They seemed to have lost all hope of a German victory, and when interrogated, gave information willingly.

An eminent medical specialist, who fell into our hands, gave an interesting description of Hitler, whom he had once met. He claimed to have discerned a diabolical personality, governed by an unbalanced, extrovert mind. He was sure that the Fuhrer would not commit suicide, but would hang on to the last to have his own complete and final "Gotterdammerung".

On the 4th of October more attacks were put in on the "Island" by Panzer and S. S. troops. Once again these attacks were held, and we were able to mount an attack in our turn in the direction of Haalderen.

A platoon of the 1th Battalion, the Hampshire Regiment, (50th Division), which took part in this, came in for some hard fighting. When the platoon commander was wounded, Sergeant S Medway, the platoon sergeant, took over command. Casualties had been high, but he quickly re-organised two sections in a shell-torn orchard, and led them on to their objective in the face of heavy fire. The Battalion on the right did not reach their objectives until after dark, but during the afternoon and evening the Platoon held on to their positions. Sergeant Medway, who had displayed great bravery and coolness throughout, was awarded the Military Medal.

On the left of the "Island" bridgehead, during the same day, the 101st US Airborne Division took over from the 43rd Division, who returned to the Nijmegen area for a short rest. Fighting flared up in this sector on October 5th and 6th, and the enemy had managed to capture the small town of Opheusden by the morning of the 6th. The 5th Battalion, the Duke of Cornwall's Light Infantry came under command of the US Airborne Division, and were attached to 502 RCT. The Battalion was employed in a counter attack on Opheusden that afternoon, and excelled themselves by their gallant fighting. The appreciation of the Americans for the good work of the Battalion is shown in the following letter from Colonel RF Sink, commanding 506 Parachute Regiment (US), to the Commanding General of the 101st US Airborne Division.

> "On the 6th October 1944 the Duke of Cornwall's Light Infantry Battalion, commanded by Lieut Colonel Taylor, was attached to 502 RCT. In the early afternoon of October 6th this Battalion was committed in an assault on the town of Opheusden, to take over a portion of the attacking front of the 1st Battalion, 506 Parachute Infantry. These troops attacked on schedule with vigour and determination in the face of withering enemy fire. The courage and ability shown by these troops was an inspiration to the 1st Battalion.

The gallantry of the British officers and men was outstanding, and instilled in the men of the 506 Parachute Infantry the highest regard for the fighting ability of the British infantry.

The undersigned desires that Lieut Colonel Taylor and his entire Battalion receive full credit for their notable work.

(Signed) R. F. Sink
Colonel.

Two days later all the troops on the "Island" came under the command of 12 Corps, and 30 Corps HQ turned its attention to planning for an attack Eastwards through the Reichswald Forest, in which it was intended that the 43rd Division should play the major part. This attack, as it was planned, never took place, but the work done was to prove very useful some three month later when the Corps started planning for the famous operation "Veritable".

During the planning it became necessary to open a route across the Maas — Waal Canal, through Hatert. The massive old bridge there had, of course, been destroyed, and the erection of a new one, in the time available, proved a difficult problem. The distance between abutments was too great for a single span Bailey bridge, and piles were not practicable. An ingenious solution was discovered, and Bailey panels were erected vertically on a floating base, the whole construction being made of standard Bailey parts.

The bridge was built by the 11th Field Company of the Royal Engineers, whose Commanding Officer, Major BS Armitage, had been largely responsible for the design. This was the first "floating tower" Bailey bridge ever constructed and a remarkable engineering achievement.

After their short rest the 43rd Division now moved down to the front facing the Reichswald Forest, where they remained until the end of October, taking part in active patrolling, and gathering useful information for the future. Weather conditions were bad, and the enemy was constantly on the alert, but the situation had its lighter moments. Movement by day was an unhealthy business, and movement by night was tricky. There were several minor casualties amongst the Despatch Riders, accompanied by a great deal of bad language, and Quartermasters experienced plenty of unaccustomed thrills as they carried supplies and letters to the forward troops through the mud and minefields.

A wary eye had to be kept open for the innumerable booby traps. Yet another type was discovered about this time in the form of mined beetroots. A charge was inserted in the centre of the beetroot, and pulling it up caused a nasty explosion.

H. M. THE KING AT 30 CORPS HQ TALKS TO OFFICERS OF THE 82ND U.S. AIRBORNE DIVISION WHO LED THE AMERICAN AIRBORNE LANDINGS AT GRAVE AND NIJMEGEN. LIEUT. GENERAL HORROCKS IS ON THE LEFT

30 Corps took over command of the "Island" again on the 18th of October. We knew that the enemy could flood the whole "Island" to a depth of several feet by blowing the banks of the Neder Rijn. It was therefore thought advisable to be prepared, and plans were made to evacuate the area should the enemy take this step. Civilians were, in fact, evacuated from certain areas by Dukws. The Dukw crews reported that the amount of furniture that these people wanted to bring with them was positively amazing. Bicycles, of course, had to come with them, but some wanted to bring large bedsteads, and even wardrobes.

In other parts of Occupied Holland the Germans had already inundated the land, and the situation was very grim for the Dutch in these localities. It was estimated that 17 per-cent of the total arable land had been flooded. The Dutch Government in London stated that the large cities were already without meat, and it was expected the supplies of bread, butter, sugar, and potatoes, would run out by the end of October. Occupied Holland was also short of fuel and light, and further, the Dutch Government estimated that in the major cities sewerage, and the main supply of drinking water, would soon cease.

All this time the town of Nijmegen was still being shelled, but entertainments went on. The possibility of a bomb or shell coming through the roof probably added to the alertness and enjoyment of the audiences. On one occasion when a woman mind-reader was doing her act, a bomb fell close by. The audience quickly pointed out to her that she might be pretty hot at forecasting people's domestic affairs, but she had omitted to forecast anything about the bomb.

Meanwhile it had been learned that a number of men of the 1st British Airborne Division were still on the other side of the Neder Rijn. On October 19th Lieut Colonel Dobie DSO of the 1st Airborne managed to cross the Neder Rijn a few miles downstream from Arnhem, and brought the news that a number of them had found shelter in Dutch homes. It was decided to attempt a rescue, and this was organised in conjunction with the 101st US Airborne Division. As it was realised that a major attack would only result in heavy casualties, it was planned to make a stealthy attempt with twenty assault boats, each manned by four Sappers of 210 Field Company RE. The two flanking boats each carried an American fighting patrol. Instructions were passed to the British Airborne troops by means of a secret telephone line to the Dutch Underground Movement in Arnhem.

Before the attempt was made the men who were to take part in it carried out extensive special training, and a rehearsal was staged on the River Maas.

On the night of the 22nd/23rd of October, with Lieut Colonel Dobie accompanied by the commander of the Americans and Major JE Weller, OC 210 Field Company in the centre boat, the plan was put into operation. Everything went well, and although there was a very strong current running, all the boats got across safely. Waiting at the agreed rendez vous were 138 officers and men of the Airborne Division. Without the enemy knowing anything at all about it all these men were brought back safely to the Southern bank.

There were several occasions when the Dutch Underground Movement themselves made daring crossings of the Waal to the West of Nijmegen, to bring back British Airborne men, or airmen, from the German zone. They proved to be particularly useful to us during the winter months. They were well organised, and well armed with British and German weapons. At first the Orange armband was their only insignia, but later we were able to supply them with British uniforms. Their units came under command of British formations, and helped to man defensive positions.

There followed a very quiet period along the whole of the Corps front and activity was restricted to patrols and intermittent shelling. The enemy were fully engaged in the South, where the Americans had pierced the Siegfried defence.

On the Reichswald front Americans from the 82nd US Airborne Division carried out noteworthy patrols, and on one occasion a one-man patrol went out and kidnapped two of the enemy from their own defence localities. Apart from the discomforture caused to the enemy by these operations, the intelligence obtained was extremely useful.

A German letter, subsequently captured, contained the following interesting little sidelight on how the Boche felt about these raids. "Here I am lying in the bushes waiting for Tommy to come along. He will get a surprise if he does come. The same applies to us, of course, if he surprises us instead."

During this period the Hun artillery fired leaflet shells into our lines on the "Island". They were of the usual type such as: "Why get maimed or killed and make your family suffer when you could easily desert and stay safe as a prisoner of war?" and "Why should English be killing Germans when both should be fighting Bolshevism?"

On the night of the 30th October an exceptionally daring patrol was carried out by six men of the 101st US Airborne Division. They crossed the Neder Rijn, and penetrated deep into enemy territory and early next morning set up an Observation Post in a house where two Germans were sleeping. They were awakened and were surprised to find that they were prisoners of the US Army. Wireless communication was established, and although the nearest regimental set was more than five miles away, reception was perfect all that day. During daylight all the members of the patrol stayed in the house, and any civilians who entered it were told that they must remain there until the morning of the 1st of November. Also during the day four German soldiers wandered into the yard and were immediately captured.

When night fell one member of the patrol remained in the house to guard the prisoners, while the other five went out on to the main Arnhem-Utrecht road, and set up a vehicle trap. In a short time the trap produced a motor-cycle, an amphibious Jeep, and a truck together with sixteen prisoners.

Picking up the sixth member of the patrol, the whole party mounted the truck, and set off with the intention of riding all the way to Renkum. The truck, however, became bogged only a mile from the OP. The Germans were lined up in columns of two, and were marched to Renkum, where they moved boldly through the streets, posing as a German platoon. On the bank of the river another ten Germans were captured from emplacements without a fight, and finally the patrol, with their prisoners, were ferried safely back across the Neder Rijn.

The British troops also did their share of these daring patrols. As an example of one of many patrols carried out, a two-man patrol from the 5th Battalion, the Duke of Cornwall's Light Infantry, consisting of Sergeant Dean, DCM, and Private Lyons, penetrated into the Reichswald Forest and spent eighteen hours there locating enemy positions. On returning at night down a track, they found their way blocked by an enemy sentry. They quickly picked up some boxes lying nearby, and, adopting the role of a German ration party, made their way past the German unchallenged, and got safely back to their headquarters.

For over a month Club Route had not moved forward and a period of static warfare seemed to have set in. But other plans were afoot for 30 Corps. The Canadian Army, having cleared the Antwerp pocket, had reached the Maas on our left, and, on November 9th, command of the "Island" was taken over by the Second Canadian Corps. Then our Divisions began to move Southwards to concentrate for the next battle.

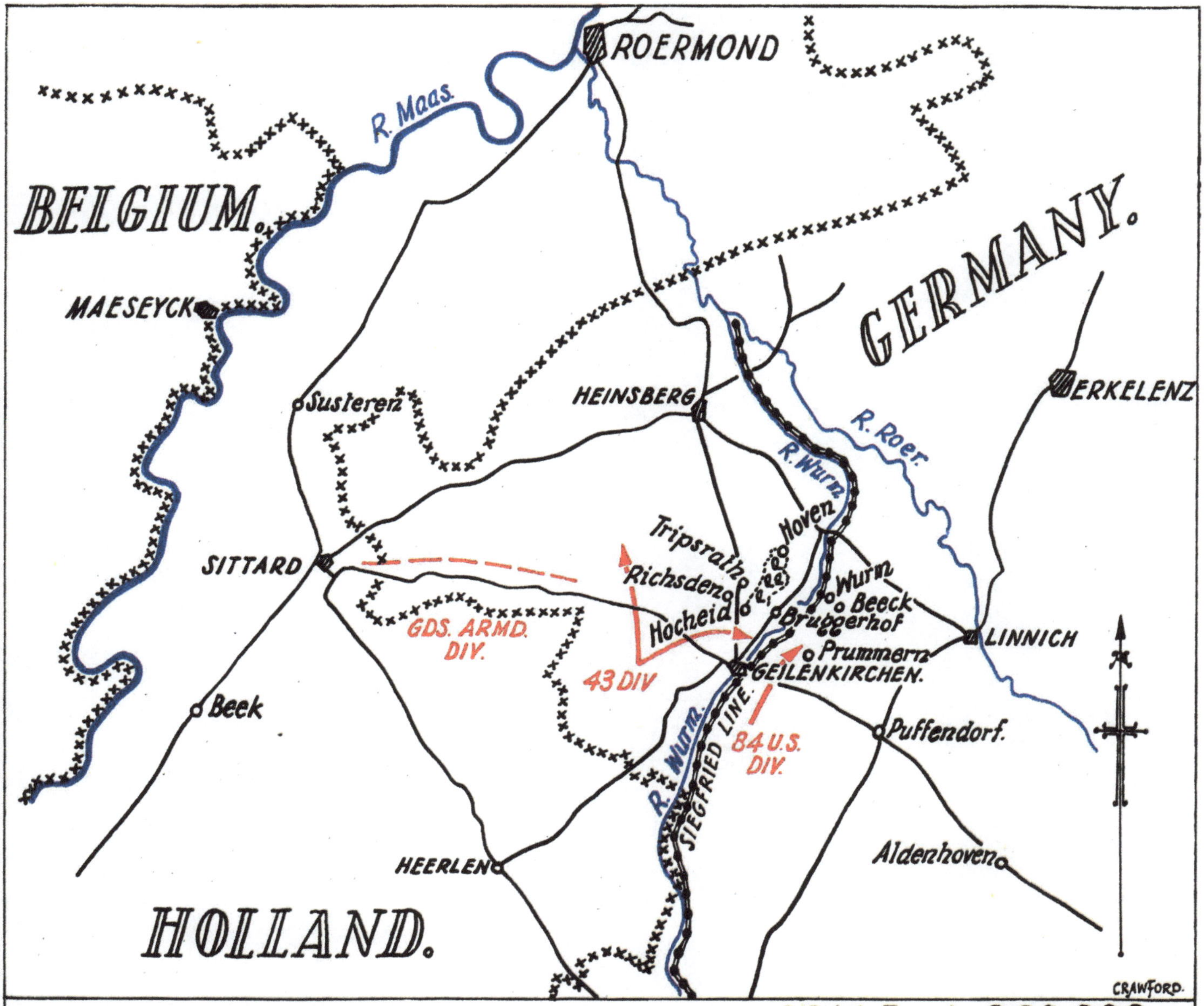

INTO THE REICH.

SCALE 1:200,000.

0 1 2 3 4 5 6 7 8 9 10

• Miles •

CHAPTER SEVEN

INTO THE REICH

The Allied Commanders were determined that the enemy should be given no chance to re-organise his battered divisions during the long winter months. Stretched to breaking point as they were, the enemy was still holding a considerable armoured force in the shape of the Sixth Panzer Army in reserve somewhere behind his front, although it was not known exactly where it was.

The enemy had already experienced the folly of committing his tanks to a battle on the wrong side of a bridge-less river (the Seine); he had a healthy respect for our bombers and their capacity for destroying bridges, and he could not afford to ignore the possibility of a repetition of the Falaise Gap if he fought an armoured battle West of the Rhine. If we could get him to do this, however, the end of the Second World War was in sight.

The Allied armies were massed along the German frontier from the Island to the Swiss frontier, while the Americans had already broken into the Siegfried Line and had captured Aachen. The German people were getting a taste of what it felt like to have the invader in their own country. Everywhere, frantic digging was taking place as new defence lines were flung up. Spades were being thrust into the hands of the Volksturm, the Hitler Youth and conscripts and they were being ordered to dig, and dig fast. Digging, and still more digging, was the order of the day.

The Americans held a bridgehead over the River Maas South of Maeseyck, where the ground takes the shape of a rough triangle (into which the uneven frontier of Germany jutted) between the rivers Maas and Roer. At the apex of this triangle the Roer flows into the Maas at Roermond, which was still in enemy hands.

It was mainly a marshy area, consisting of meadows and ploughland, woods and orchards. After rain the going became sticky and promised trouble for our tanks, especially as the weather was consistently bad from November to February.

30 Corps took over this bridgehead from the Americans on November 12th, and, by the 15th, the 43rd Division and the Guards Armoured Division had taken over the sectors allotted to them from the American formations. The 50th Division, who had been with us so long, had been left behind on the "Island", and was to fight with 30 Corps no more.

On our right flank the Americans were to thrust towards Cologne, and, to assist the Ninth US Army in getting over the Roer at Linnich, 30 Corps was to capture the vital road centre of Geilenkirchen.

The River Wurm flows sluggishly through this little industrial town. Apart from its characteristic muddiness the river had another distinction, for, coming North from Aachen, along the ridge to the East of the river, and proceeding North East to where the Wurm empties itself into the Roer, just above Heinsberg, was established the much vaunted Siegfried Line. It was thought, however, that there were only a few individual strong-points facing South East, and that the town would therefore be vulnerable to attack from this direction.

For this operation, in addition to the two British Divisions already mentioned, the 84th American Infantry Division, the 113th US Cavalry Group, the British 8th Armoured Brigade, and four squadrons of the specialist 79th Armoured Division, were under command of 30 Corps.

The Corps Commander decided to encircle Geilenkirchen by an attack from the North West by the 43rd Division, and an attack from the South East by the 84th US Division, who were to clear the pill-boxes of the Siegfried Line. The American infantry were then to capture Geilenkirchen, and, finally, the 43rd Division was to exploit to the high ground South of Heinsberg. The full weight of the Corps artillery and rocket-firing Typhoons of the RAF were to support each phase of the attack.

The big joint Allied offensive opened on November 15th when 12 Corps on our left began to push forward towards the Maas. At noon the following day the Americans began their new offensive into the Rhine Province, and, on the 18th, 30 Corps joined the battle.

The Americans attacked at dawn with a combat team supported by the Sherwood Rangers Yeomanry of the 8th Armoured Brigade and elements of 79th Armoured Division and made good progress. The attack was heralded by terrific artillery fire. An inferno of vivid orange flashes stabbed the sky and the ground shook with the crash of the heavy, medium and field guns all opening up at the same moment. The enemy artillery replied, but his answer was a feeble one compared to our terrific barrage. A tremendous weight of metal was hitting the German front-line positions, and an added attraction for our gunners was the knowledge that their shells were not destroying French, Belgian or Dutch homes any longer, but were now falling on the Reich itself. At last we were beginning to repay the Hun for the trail of devastation he had left behind through the countries of Europe.

The concrete pill-boxes of the Siegfried Line caused some trouble to the Americans for the enemy manning these pill-boxes remained inside until our tanks had passed, and then rushed out to occupy foxholes from which they engaged our on-coming infantry. This trick was, however, soon discovered, and our tanks, whipping round, came back and did great slaughter.

By evening the village of Prummern had been captured and American patrols were pushing forward to the Wurm valley.

Meanwhile, shortly after midday, the 43rd Division began its assault. This went well and by evening all objectives had been taken. Between them the two Divisions had captured over 800 prisoners and patrols from each had linked up in the Wurm valley, thus completing the encirclement of Geilenkirchen.

It was a company of the Duke of Cornwall's Light Infantry, under Major Holland MC, that cut the road behind the town, and for a long time the enemy were unaware of their presence. They had the satisfaction of destroying several ammunition wagons, captured thirty prisoners and shot up several small enemy detachments. Eventually, after a successful ambush of two SP guns, the enemy tumbled to the fact that our men were behind them, and then they counter-attacked viciously with tanks and SS infantry. After a hard battle at close quarters the counter-attack was beaten off, and, shortly afterwards, American troops joined up with them.

A company of the 1st Battalion of the Worcestershire Regiment led the attack on Richsden and Tripsrath. The tanks of the 4th/7th Dragoon Guards, supporting the Battalion, were having a bad time and many of them were bogged. Major JD Ricketts, who was commanding the leading company, organised fire support for the attack on Richsden from a platoon of another Battalion, then, finding one tank which had managed to survive the mud he ordered the commander of it to support the attack. He returned to his company, and, moving with the leading platoon, led them into Richsden in the face of intense enemy fire.

The village immediately came under heavy fire from mortars and guns in the Siegfried Line and the commanding officer of the Battalion was wounded. Major Ricketts took command of the Battalion, and, after reorganising his men, led the attack on the next objective, Tripsrath. The enemy put up a stiff resistance which was finally overcome, and, although there were counter-attacks, they were all repulsed. Major Ricketts, who had been under constant, heavy fire all day, was a great inspiration and example to his men. He was awarded the DSO for his part in these attacks.

The country around Geilenkirchen may have been beautiful once, but now it was a horrible scene of desolation, for very few houses had escaped destruction. The civilians had all been evacuated by the Germans and had left pitiful evidence of their hurried departure. Remnants of hurried meals were left on the half-wrecked tables and frightened pigs, poultry and cattle wandered about the battle-swept roads. Sometimes, these latter unfortunate creatures helped us, if not themselves, by stepping on a mine and thus revealing the presence of a mine-field.

Smashed as Geilenkirchen was, however, nearly every building had a substantial cellar, and these provided some sort of protection. They had given shelter to the Germans during our barrages, enabling them to fight again when our infantry appeared, and they now gave shelter to our own men from the very active and uncomfortably accurate Hun artillery in the Siegfried Line.

During that night our tanks had many misfortunes trying to manoeuvre in the soft ground. The 8th Armoured Brigade alone had 23 tanks bogged and the crews had a rough time endeavouring to get their vehicles out of the quagmire under the heavy shellfire.

After the attack on Tripsrath a number of casualties from the tanks were stranded in the forward positions as it was considered too dangerous to evacuate them owing to the enemy's observation of the road. The Chaplain of the 4th/7th Dragoon Guards, the Rev Mark Green, volunteered to fetch them in, and, going forward in a light tank, he collected the wounded men under heavy shellfire and brought them back. He went up the next day to Richsden, where there were more casualties, and these he brought back safely. His gallantry was an inspiration to everyone and he was awarded the Military Cross for his initiative and bravery.

It had been intended to use the flail tanks of the 79th Armoured Division to clear the minefields but once again the soggy ground beat us and most of the flails became stuck. Consequently, our tanks tried to break through the still unswept minefields, but as some were disabled by the mines and others became bogged only a very few managed to get through to support the infantry.

A troop of tanks of the Sherwood Rangers Yeomanry, under the command of Sergeant HCL Douthwaite, had supported the US infantry during their attack on Prummern. Owing to the bad state of the ground and the extremely heavy shelling the infantry

A MEMBER OF A TANK CREW PICKS HIS WAY THROUGH THE MUD AT GEILENKIRCHEN TO GET WATER FOR TEA

were unable to bring up their anti-tank guns and consolidate. During the night, Sergeant Douthwaite positioned himself in the centre of the village, within two hundred yards of enemy infantry and guns. With only two tanks left he had to guard the four roads leading into the centre of Prummern, and, during the night, he drove off two attacks by German Bazooka teams by dismounted action. Hearing an enemy tank approaching the Sergeant placed some German mines on the road, and these successfully disabled the enemy tank. He then got round to the rear of it and set it on fire. Two attempts by the enemy to counter-attack the American infantry were broken up by offensive action on the part of Sergeant Douthwaite, and he was later awarded the Military Medal for his gallant part in the action.

If tank movement had been difficult on the first day of the battle, by the second day the continuous rain had made it practically impossible. Progress by the infantry could not be rapid because of the multitudinous mines and booby traps. Gradually, however, they overcame the difficulties and cleared the enemy from Geilenkirchen according to plan. The German garrison fled North East along the Wurm valley road, and ran into a hail of fire from our tanks and infantry who were blocking the road and sitting along the sides of the valley. They suffered heavy casaulties and over 200 of them were taken prisoner.

When our attack began, the second-rate 183rd Peoples Grenadier Division was opposing our troops and it had been badly mauled. On the second day, our old enemies the 15th Panzer Grenadier Division made their appearance and launched several counter-attacks against the 84th US Division. These were all beaten off and proved costly to the enemy, and, in one attack alone, the Americans accounted for six enemy tanks.

On November 19th the 43rd Division attacked and cleared the Hocheid Woods. This attack was planned at great speed, and it was not possible to make a reconnaissance either of the start line or the forming up point. The attack was made by two companies of the 7th Battalion the Somerset Light Infantry, and four field regiments of artillery put down a creeping barrage in front of the advancing troops. In spite of the rapid planning all went well, and, within an hour, the leading companies were in their appointed places, but, then, the real difficulties began.

There was only one muddy, sloping path by which even tracked vehicles could reach the forward companies, and this, in parts, was in full view of the enemy. The path, flanked by deep ditches on either side, was extremely slippery and treacherous. The vehicles of the Commanding Officer and the RA Battery Commander were quickly ditched, and that night, when attempts were made, to get anti-tank guns, carriers and food up to the companies, the toll of the ditch quickly mounted. The track soon became quite impassable, and food, greatcoats and blankets had to be carried on foot through a thousand yards of wood which was under heavy shellfire.

Stretcher bearers had a difficult time. Soon after the attack went in, two of them, Lance Corporal Barrell and Bandsman Board, were called forward to attend to two German snipers who had been located and wounded. They dressed their wounds and then found that our infantry had advanced out of sight. They tried to link up with them, but, in the dark, thick woods they lost their way, and finally ran into a party of five Panzer Grenadiers who took them prisoner.

Determined to get away if they could, they tried their powers of persuasion on the Grenadiers. After a long argument, during which they emphasised that their job was saving life and not killing, and that there were others lying around in the woods who would perhaps die unless they received medical attention, they were allowed to go. Unable to find their way back to our lines they eventually took refuge among some straw bales in a clearing of the wood where they spent an uncomfortable night with the shells of both sides passing overhead, and, as usual, the rain pouring down.

The next morning they made their way to a village, which they found to be in enemy hands, and took shelter in an empty cellar, in which the German uniforms, helmets and ammunition which they found did little to increase their confidence. Even when the village was captured by our own troops their troubles were not over, for the Americans who took it ignored their yells of "English!" and "Red Cross!" and passed them down a grenade. The few seconds before it exploded must have been the worst and longest in their lives. By great good fortune, it was a blast grenade, and they were not injured, and finally they managed to convince the Americans that they really were English. This instance shows that a stretcher-bearer's life is one of the most difficult and dangerous in an infantry battalion.

On November 20th both Divisions spent the day consolidating and mopping up the area, and more counter-attacks were repulsed. The fighting had been sharp and the enemy obviously bitterly resented this intrusion into the "Sacred Soil of the Reich", but all our objectives had been gained and held under terrible weather conditions.

During this day another 250 prisoners were taken, bringing the total Corps 'bag' since the operation began to over 1,300. It was about this time that the first prisoner from the much-heralded

Volksturm was captured. He was 17 years old and had had only two and a half weeks military training. He wore an Italian overcoat, Wehrmacht blouse and trousers, and carried a French rifle. Said he, with pardonable pride: "I stayed in the foxhole until I was captured, while the other men from my company ran away at the sight of the enemy." A German officer who was captured was quite convinced that Hitler was mad. He had a favourite story of the little girl who asked her mother: "Mummy, will the big lunatic chew up our carpets, too?"

Meanwhile, in Hocheid Woods, the Somersets had dragged their anti-tank guns into position through the mud, and were holding on grimly under the unpleasant conditions. The memory of those woods has left an indelible impression on the minds of those who were there. The gloom of the darkening trees, the constant dripping rain and sodden ground, the roofed dug-outs which, in spite of the roofs, had always at least six inches of water on the floor, were only some of the discomforts which Nature provided. Even more discomforting was the enemy shellfire, for the Germans had that wood registered accurately from every angle.

One soldier was asked if Hocheid was worse than Normandy.

"No", he said, after deliberation, "I would not care to say anything was worse than Chateau de Fontaine, but it was certainly bad."

The Anti-tank Platoon headquarters of the Somersets considered themselves lucky to have a small cellar under a house in the village of Hocheid. Unfortunately for them, however, the crew of a Sherman tank decided that it would be better covered if they pushed its 17 pounder gun through one window of this house and fired out through the other. This they did, and they fired one shot, the terrific muzzle blast bringing the whole house down in a dusty roar of rubble. The members of the platoon headquarters, when they had recovered from the shock, came up to the surface and announced their views of the tank crew in no uncertain manner, while Captain Townshend, the Platoon Commander, traced the tank crew's ancestry back a long, long way, both individually and collectively.

When the anti-tank gunners came to be relieved it was found to be impossible to move the guns owing to the saturated state of the ground, and they remained in the same positions, and were cleaned and fired by successive units, until the Corps left the area.

The next two days, the 21st and 22nd, saw bitter fighting to the East of the River Wurm, where the 84th US Division attempted to capture the villages of Wurm and Beeck. They met with fierce opposition from the Panzer Grenadiers, and, although not a great deal of progress was made, by the end of the second day the American infantry had reached the outskirts of Beeck, but were held up there by fire from the Siegfried pill-boxes.

On the left, a company of the 5th Battalion, the Duke of Cornwall's Light Infantry, penetrated into the village of Hoven, at the North end of the Hocheid Woods, and consolidated their position. In the early hours of the following morning they were attacked by enemy fighting patrols. These attacks were repulsed, but, later in the morning, it was observed that a strong German infantry force was forming up for a bigger attack. The Company Commander, Major MR Lonsdale, ordered fire to be held until the Huns were within eighty yards. This was done, and a great number of the enemy were caught in this fire trap and wiped out. A further attack was also repulsed and a S. P. gun was knocked out by a P. I. A. T.

Soon afterwards the company HQ received a direct hit, but our men continued to take a big toll of the enemy, at a heavy cost to themselves. After two further attacks had been made and beaten off, it was obvious that they would either have to surrender or fight their way out, as most of the company were either killed or wounded and ammunition was getting very low. The Huns were closing in on all sides, and, finally, Major Lonsdale decided to cut his way out with the seventeen unwounded men still remaining.

This they succeeded in doing, and, after a fierce action, they arrived safely back at Battalion HQ with their fire power reduced to half a magazine of Bren gun ammunition, and two rounds of Sten. Two enemy deserters later complained bitterly of the fierce resistance which this company had put up at Hoven. Major Lonsdale was awarded the DSO for his part in this gallant action.

Counter-attacks continued throughout the next day, the 23rd, some of which achieved success at first, but in all cases the situation was later restored. The Corps now had a firm grip on Geilenkirchen, the original objective of the operation, and, with the battle turning to the defensive, the 84th US Division reverted to the command of 13 US Corps.

There followed a period of inactivity on the Corps front, broken only by an incident at Tripsrath. A strong party of enemy troops was still holding out in a school building at the Northern end of the village, and the 5th Battalion of the Wiltshire Regiment cleared this strongpoint after a short artillery bombardment. They rushed in as soon as the artillery lifted and before the Germans had time to leave their shelters, and, by doing so, accounted for all the enemy and took fifty prisoners.

Our Divisions were now between two flooded rivers. Behind them was the Maas, the water level of which was approximately one and a half metres above normal for the time of the year, and which had, in several places, overflowed its banks. All the pontoon bridges were put out of action with the exception of one American bridge, and the current was too strong to allow Dukws to be used to carry supplies across. In front of our troops was the flooded Roer. It was known that excessive flooding of this river was controlled by the dams South of Duren, and these were in enemy hands. It was to be expected that the Germans would either destroy these dams or at least open the sluice gates to delay our advance.

On the 30th of November the Corps was visited by Field Marshal Sir Bernard Montgomery, who saw the troops in action on the newly captured German soil. He visited forward positions and decorated men of the Corps.

Meanwhile, the mud was getting steadily worse, and supplying the forward troops proved a tremendous difficulty. The real life-savers of the situation were the Weasels, which, with their wide, lightly built tracks and high metal sides were able to slide over the mud with considerable success. Even so, their casaulty rate was very heavy and REME workshops were kept fully employed.

The Corps Commander now decided to form an Infantry Battalion out of Corps Service personnel to relieve the infantry in the line and enable them to get as much rest as possible. It consisted of a small headquarters found by 30 Corps HQ, and four companies made up of RASC personnel from the Guards Armoured Division, the 43rd Division and 30 Corps Troops RASC, and of REME 30 Corps.

The Battalion was formed on the 29th of November, and, after spending two days getting into shape, relieved the 7th Battalion of the Somerset Light Infantry in the line on the 1st of December. As there were no trained anti-tank gunners it was necessary to call on the Somersets to leave their own guns and personnel in position. Shortly afterwards, when the 52nd Lowland Division and the 7th Armoured Division came under command of 30 Corps, it was possible to form two further RASC Companies. For nearly three weeks the Services Battalion did excellent relief work, and every RASC driver and REME mechanic who served in it was proud in the knowledge that he had been able to take some of the burden off the shoulders of his infantry friends.

A squadron of the 43rd Reconnaissance Regiment was holding the extreme right hand position of the Corps which consisted of a group of posts around the shattered farmstead of Bruggerhof. From here the ground sloped down to the River Wurm, and beyond that was the long ridge crowned by the pill-boxes of the Siegfried Line. The farmstead was a favourite target for the German gunners who gave it a daily pasting.

The long nights were a terrible strain for the forward posts. The slit tranches had to be manned before five o'clock in the evening and stand down was not until eight o'clock in the morning. Eyes and ears were constantly straining to pick up movement, for the German patrols were very active.

One German patrol approached a slit trench where Sergeant Reeves and two men of the 43rd Reconnaissance Regiment were manning a Bren gun. The sergeant pulled the trigger, but for some reason the gun did not fire. He re-cocked and tried again, but still the gun failed to fire. The leading German rushed up to the trench and sprayed the inside with his automatic pistol, wounding one of the men, but Sergeant Reeves calmly recocked his Bren, and the third time it fired. It was only just in time. Two of the Huns were killed, and the rest of the patrol fled, pursued by a hail of fire. For his coolness and perseverance under these trying circumstances Sergeant Reeves received the Military Medal.

Artificial moonlight, or Monty's Moonlight as the men called it, helped a good deal during these long, dark nights. This was provided by searchlights directed along the ground from the rear towards the enemy positions.

The German prisoners captured had very divergent views on the value of this moonlight. Some claimed that it was an advantage to them as it gave them a larger field of vision, made movement easier, and prevented would-be deserters crossing to our lines. Others, however, said it was distinctly disadvantageous as the shadows thrown were unnatural and misleading, and our patrols could use it as cover. Others, again, said that it dazzled them and that they felt they could not move without being seen, at a time when, normally, free movement would have been possible.

On December 3rd the news came through that our old hunting ground, the "Island", now held by British and Canadian units had at last been flooded by the Germans. This may have damped the ground, but it did not damp the Canadians' spirits. One party of Canadians, surrounded, heard a German NCO call out: "You English gentlemen had better surrender."

They replied: "We ain't English — we ain't gentlemen — and we ain't gonna surrender." They did not.

Meanwhile, 30 Corps had been planning for an operation which was to clear the enemy from all the ground South West of the River Roer. The planning was completed and the artillery programme prepared, but our Corps did not proceed with the operation, for December 13th, 12 Corps took over all the formations under our command, and the conduct of the battle.

Then, in the greatest secrecy, with formation signs on all vehicles blacked out, and the famous Corps flash removed, Corps Headquarters moved back into Holland to re-plan an assault on the Reichswald.

It was not intended that the enemy should know where 30 Corps had disappeared to, for, by now, he had learnt that the presence of the rampant boar in any locality heralded an impending attack.

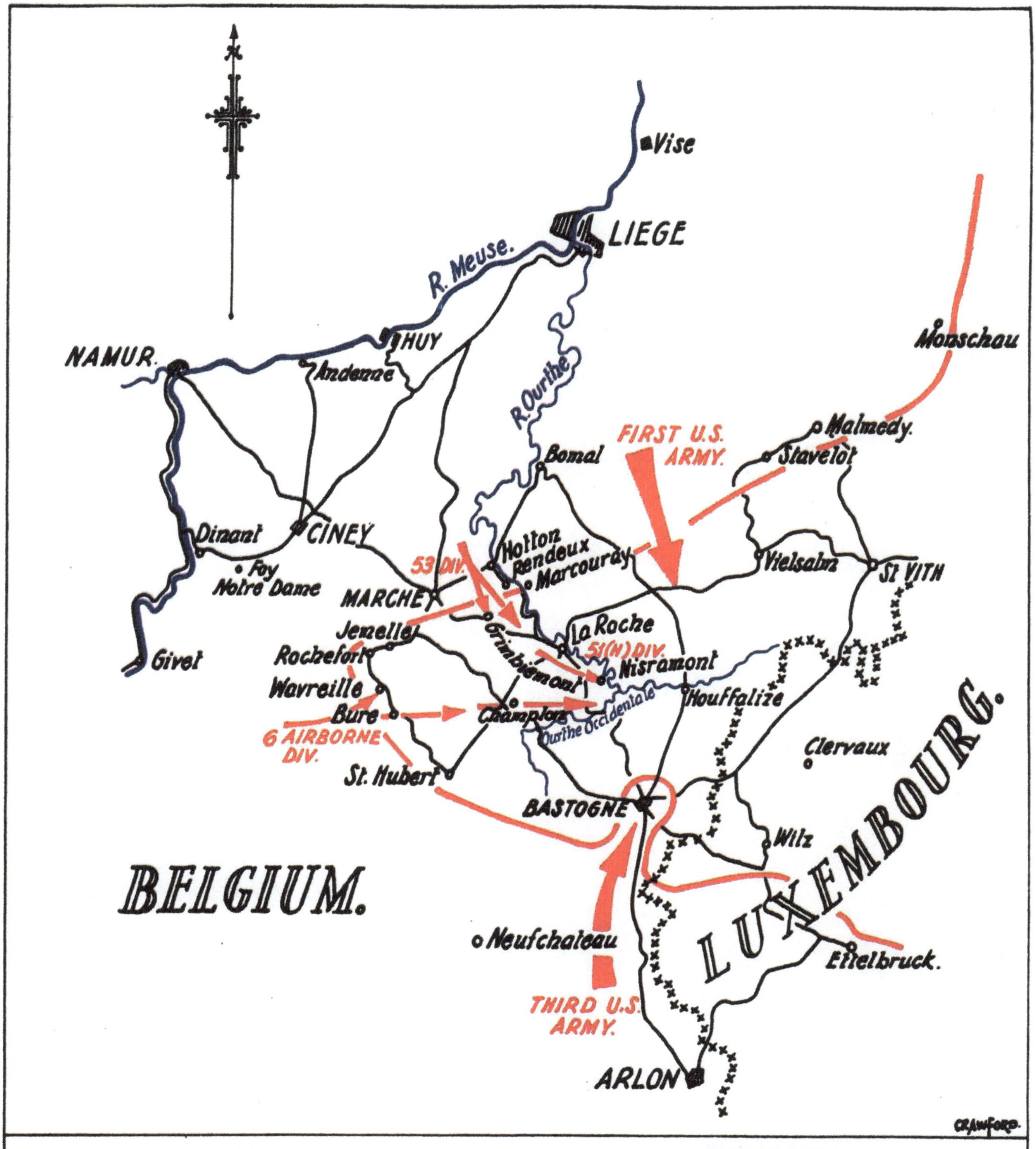

THE AFFAIR IN THE ARDENNES.

ALLIED LINE AT 28 DEC......

SCALE 1: 700,000.

10 5 0 10 20

· Miles ·

CHAPTER EIGHT

THE AFFAIR IN THE ARDENNES

n December 16th the Germans surprised the Allies by launching an offensive in the Ardennes. For some time the weather had been very bad and air reconnaissance consequently very much restricted. As a result, the enemy had been able to move his troops into new positions without our knowledge. Furthermore, he unexpectedly threw his tanks into sectors which were considered not suitable for armour.

The attacks were launched at five different points along a seventy mile front, and were initially light, having the appearance merely of reconnaissance in force, and it was not until the night of the 16th/17th that the Germans showed their hand completely and used airborne forces, making their greatest air effort since Normandy.

Parachutists were dropped over a wide area stretching from North of Aachen to Malmedy. The enemy now threw his full weight into the battle along two main axes. It was later ascertained that the plan was for one force to drive through Malmedy to Liege to cut off the First and Ninth American Armies and secure a position along the Meuse. Once that was accomplished the drive would be made towards Antwerp to take this vital port from the Allies, and to cut off the British and Canadian forces in Holland from the rest of the Allied forces. The Southern drive was to go straight through to the Meuse at Dinant and Namur, and hold the Southern flank.

It was a bold plan, and evidently the Germans' last effort at a major offensive in the West. It was heralded by inspiring exhortations from the German Army Commanders.

"Soldiers of the Fatherland, the hour has struck. Strong attacking armies are advancing. Everything is at stake, every man must do his holy duty and make superhuman efforts for the Fatherland," urged von Rundstedt.

"We will not disappoint our Fuhrer and Fatherland, who created the Sword of Retribution. Our battle is now on, and no soldier in the world must be better than ourselves" boasted Model.

Good advice was given, too, as a captured order dated December 16th showed:

"If you are brave, industrious and resourceful, you will ride in American vehicles and eat good American food. If, however, you are stupid, cowardly, and lack initiative, you will walk, cold and hungry, all the way to the Channel".

The parachutists' role was mainly diversionary, and most of them were quickly mopped up, only those in the South being fortunate enough to link up with the advancing forces.

In addition to the bona fide warriors dropped from the air, the Germans dropped some American speaking Huns dressed in American uniform, and these caused considerable confusion and scares for some time. However, there were occasions when they confused themselves, too. It is reported that one of them, seeing the futility of it all, walked up to the first American he could find and shouted, "I surrender!" The other replied, "I regret, but I also am a German and wish to surrender". Their wishes were soon complied with.

On the 17th, the 1st SS Panzer Corps by-passed Malmedy, two other Panzer Divisions encircled St Vith, and another captured Clervaux. It was on this day that an appalling massacre of American prisoners of war took place. Men of the 285th Field Artillery Observation Battery were in convoy near Malmedy when they ran into a number of enemy tanks. In the ensuing action, some escaped, but about 120 Americans were taken prisoner, robbed of their valuables, and then lined up, six deep, in a nearby field.

Then, for no apparent reason, one of the guards fired shots into the group, and immediately afterwards two of the tanks opened fire with their machine guns. Some of the men simulated death, but many of these were shot by German soldiers. About 25 made a run for it, and 15 finally got away in spite of being wounded. It is difficult to understand the mentality of men who could countenance such senseless slaughter as this.

On the 18th, attempts to get into Malmedy were frustrated by the troops of the First US Army, but, to the South, Panzer spearheads reached Stavelot, where they met gallant and determined opposition from the men of the 82nd US Airborne Division. The enemy made more gains round St Vith, and, penetrating between Bastogne and Houffalize, cut off Bastogne from the South by crossing the Arlon — Bastogne road.

Meanwhile, 30 Corps had been planning for their next operation in the little Dutch town of Boxtel. With the German advances in the Ardennes assuming serious proportions, it was not to be expected that 30 Corps would long be out of the battle, and at six o'clock in the evening of December 19th, 30 Corps received orders to move South, with the Guards Armoured Division, the 43rd Division, and the 53rd Division under command. Five hours later 30 Corps Headquarters abandoned its planning and left Boxel to take its part in throwing back the Germans.

Field Marshal Sir Bernard Montgomery was now in command of all forces North of the breakthrough, and on December 20th he gave 30 Corps the task of dealing with any enemy crossings of the Meuse.

Accordingly, it was decided to place a strong recce screen along the Meuse from Huy to Vise, and that day the armoured cars of the 43rd Reconnaissance Regiment and the Household Cavalry made a dash to the river, and sent back detailed reports on the situation at the bridges.

The 53rd Division took up a defensive position on the River Dyle so as to block any German advance towards Brussels, while the Guards Armoured Division and the 43rd Division were positioned on their left flank ready to pounce on any Germans who succeeded in crossing the Meuse. The 51st Division, which now came under the command of the Corps, was held in reserve.

By the 21st December, enemy Panzer units had penetrated to Samree, La Roche, and Marcourt, but all their efforts to capture Malmedy had been frustrated. A magnificent defence was being put up by the men of the 101st US Airborne Division in beleagured Bastogne, and all the heavy attacks put in against them by 116th Panzer Division were thrown back with heavy losses to the enemy.

The Airborne boys in Bastogne received an ultimatum from the Germans. It was formally addressed to "The USA Commander of the encircled town of Bastogne", and was rather long-winded. Extracts stated:

"The fortune of war is changing. In this town the USA forces have been encircled by strong German armoured units. There is only one way to save the USA troops from total annihilation, and that is the honourable surrender of the encircled town. In order to think it over, a term of two hours is granted, at the end of which, if this proposal should be rejected, one German Artillery Corps, and six ack ack battalions, are ready to annihilate the USA troops".

The Americans' reply was brief, but to the point.

"To the German Commander.

Nuts!

From the American Commander".

The Germans had driven into Luxembourg and captured Ettlebruck, but their further advance towards the capital was being held up.

On the 21st December, the 29th Armoured Brigade was placed under the command of the 53rd Division and moved down the river along the line Givet — Dinant — Namur.

Stavelot had fallen, but the Americans were resisting fiercely at Monschau, stopping the enemy's drive to Liege, while the gallant defence of Bastogne was hindering the enemy's advance along the Southern axis. This magnificent resistance by the Americans could, by now, be said to have destroyed all hopes of the enemy to "bounce" the Meuse crossings.

The next day, territorial gains by the enemy were not so great, although their attacks were still as fierce as ever. Stavelot was regained by an American counter-attack, but the Germans captured St Vith from the 7th US Armoured Division, which fell back to the North West. A force of twenty tanks of the 1st SS Panzer Division were trapped in La Gleize and wiped out. Bastogne, still holding out, was bypassed, the enemy moving round South of the town.

During the day, Van de Heydte, who trained the Parachute force used in this offensive, was captured. Thinking that Monschau was in German hands, he walked into the town and was gratefully picked up by the Americans. Van de Heydte was an old opponent, with battle experiences stretching back to Alamein, and who had fought in Normandy and on the Albert and the Meuse — Escaut Canals. Captivity, added to his trench feet and pneumonia, did nothing to restore his cheerfulness.

Now that the threat to break out towards Brussels had been reduced, 30 Corps was given the task of preventing the enemy crossing the Meuse between Givet and Vise.

The next day, December 23rd, the weather cleared up. It had previously been much too bad for effective air co-operation, a factor which had greatly helped the enemy, but this morning brought clear skies, and the Allied Air Forces were soon in the air. Fighters, fighter bombers, and bombers began to swarm over the roads used by the enemy, and his armour, equipment and transport, both motorised and horse-drawn, began to take a severe beating. The poor horses must have wished they were back in their Rest Camp, which, a prisoner reported, was situated at Drei Muehlen. He added, rather cynically, perhaps, that a Butcher Company was also located there.

The effect of the air support was soon apparent, for the enemy's offensive was brought almost to a standstill. On the 24th, the Germans seem to have realised that to get to Liege was impossible, and switched the main effort towards Namur. Patrols from the 5th Panzer Army almost reached the river at Dinant. 29th Armoured Brigade, who were patrolling in that area, had several fierce skirmishes and knocked out five enemy tanks. St Hubert fell, and the enemy pushed on towards Givet. Since the start of his offensive, he had broken through to a depth of fifty miles.

Probably the greatest tragedy of this German attack was the fact that so many Belgians, so recently liberated, were now in German hands again. In Bande, a village a few miles South of Marche, it was later ascertained, the inhabitants were ordered to hand in all Allied flags, and these were then publicly burned. It was in Bande that some German soldiers had been shot, the previous September, by some Belgian patriots, and the Germans now took a drastic revenge.

On Christmas Eve, 35 men were beaten up and then taken to a lonely, burnt-out house. The men were forced to enter one by one, and, as they did so, a Gestapo official shot them through the head. Many other distressing incidents such as this were reported. Near Stavelot, SS men shot and then burnt about 30 civilians.. It had been an unhappy break-through for our Belgian allies.

Christmas Day dawned clear, promising the Allied Air Forces another good day's hunting. The 71st Infantry Brigade took over from the 29th Armoured Brigade, who were now free to operate East of the Meuse. They quickly re-established contact with the enemy, and during the morning the 3rd Royal Tank Regiment was fighting in the area of Foy Notre Dame, and knocked out half a dozen enemy vehicles and two Panthers, and captured 100 prisoners from the 2nd Panzer Division. The American Air Force celebrated Christmas Day by destroying 811 MT vehicles, 94 AFVs and 27 enemy aircraft. In addition, enemy troops forming up for attacks were smashed from the air time and time again.

The Corps newspaper, "The Courier", brought out a special Christmas number of six pages, complete with short stories, cartoons and poems. Production of this had been a touch-and-go affair, owing to the rapid changes of location of Corps Headquarters during the week before Christmas. However, thanks to the efforts of Captain Pearson, the Editor, and the production staff, Lance Corporal Bates and Private Withams, the popular Christmas number was completed late on Christmas Eve. The "Corps Courier" had been in production since the first week in Normandy, and by now the circulation was rising towards 1,500.

Field Marshal Model did not forget his troops on Christmas Day, as an Order of the Day captured later showed. In it, he said, "Christmas is the day of peace on earth. Our enemies do not want peace, they desire the destruction and doom of our nation. For this reason we must enforce peace by the sword". The festive spirit was abroad.

Responsibility for the Meuse crossings was taken from the 71st Infantry Brigade by the 1st Brigade of the 6th Airborne Division, newly arrived from England, which now came under the command of 30 Corps, on the 26th December.

The German thrust which had cut the Ciney — Dinant road was finally and decisively smashed and mopped up on the 27th December, as part of the 2nd Panzer Division was caught at Celles, having run out of petrol. This was the first real defeat of the enemy on the Corps front since the Ardennes battle began. The strong battle group of the 2nd Panzer Division found in Celles was engaged by the 2nd US Armoured Division acting in co-operation with our 29th Armoured Brigade. In the ensuing battle, 110 vehicles and 24 AFVs were brewed up, and over 1500 prisoners were taken. This action caused the 2nd Panzer Division to withdraw towards Rochefort, and, consequently, the immediate threat to the Meuse was removed.

On the same day, 43rd Division moved East to Maastricht where it came under the command of 12 Corps.

The enemy had hoped to capture large dumps of American petrol during his advance, but this had not happened, and this fact, coupled with the terrific battering from the air that he had received on his lines of communication, would, no doubt, lead to further incidents such as the one at Celles.

Meanwhile, the gallant defence of Bastogne continued. The fighting there on Christmas Day had been particularly bitter, and no less than four divisions were now deployed against the men of the 101st US Airborne Division, who, quite undaunted by the odds, took a heavy toll of enemy tanks and infantry.

Relief, however, was on the way, for coming North from Arlon was the 4th US Armoured Division. This Division, pushing forward against the hard fighting Germans, reached the outskirts of Bastogne on the 27th, and on the 28th the town was relieved. The importance of the splendid stand at Bastogne cannot be overrated. It had forced the Germans to divert vital forces in an attempt to reduce the town. Its capture would have been invaluable to them, not only as a communications centre, but also as a firm base from which they might have resisted the advance of the Third US Army which was now driving North, spear-headed by the 4th Armoured Division.

Meanwhile, coming up from the South, French and American patrols were near St Hubert.

Although it was obvious by now that their great plan had

failed, the Germans were still ready to exploit it, and air reconnaissance reported considerable enemy movement from the West, so further big attacks were to be expected.

In the Third US Army sector, a company took billets for their men in a town. Sentries were posted, but next day no communication could be established with the company. A patrol was sent to investigate, but no trace of the men could be found beyond a few letters belonging to them which were found in the streets. It was suspected that German sympathisers had "put the finger" on the sentries and then guided German patrols to the billets where the men were sleeping.

During the next few days there was little sign of enemy aggression on the Corps front. The excellent bombing efforts of the Allied Air Forces, and the grim resistance of the American ground forces, had undoubtedly turned the tide of battle in our favour.

With the beginning of the New Year, the Allies turned to the offensive in a big way. It was planned to make a joint attack from the North and South respectively with the First and Third US Armies, both aimed at the important road centre of Houffalize. To narrow the front of the First US Army, Field Marshal Sir Bernard Montgomery ordered 30 Corps to take over the sector from Hotton to just South of Bure. The Corps Commander therefore placed the 53rd Welsh Divison on the sector Hotton-Rochefort, while two American Divisions sidestepped to the East to make room for them. The 6th Airborne Division, with 29th Armoured Brigade under command, was to attack on a general axis from Givet to St Hubert. The 30 Corps attack was to be made in unison with the attack by the First US Army.

It was on New Year's Day that the Germans put in a remarkable and unexpected attack on all our main aerodromes. Probably exasperated by the successful attacks of the Allied Airforces in the Ardennes during the past week, the enemy flung in a full-hearted Luftwaffe effort in an attempt to prevent us taking further advantage of the spell of flying weather. It was estimated that at least 800 sorties were flown by the German Air Force, but the attacks cost them dear, for over 150 enemy aircraft were destroyed.

By the morning of January 3rd, however, the weather had become our worst enemy. We attacked on this day in a driving blizzard. Snow was falling continuously and the roads were icebound. Consequently, little progress was made, although the 6th Airborne Division reached the outskirts of Bure, where the 13th Parachute Battalion and the 3rd Royal Tank Regiment became engaged in heavy fighting. Further North, at Wavreille, the 7th Parachute Battalion gained a footing in the town.

The approaches to Wavreille were reconnoitred by two troops of the 61st Reconnaissance Regiment under the command of Lieutenant MA Urban-Smith and Lieutenant W Flint. They had with them a section of the Belgian Special Air Service mounted in Jeeps and bristling with machine guns. This section was commanded by a sergeant who was a Belgian nobleman and who owned most of the land over which they were operating. Consequently, he was most anxious to assist in the expulsion of the Huns. Halfway to their objective they spotted some Germans coming up behind. They quickly opened fire, and those who survived as quickly surrendered.

Slogging on through the snow and sleet, they reached the outskirts of Wavreille and immeditely became violently engaged with the enemy. Aided by the Belgians they drove the enemy from the village, but they were counter-attacked strongly, and it became necessary for the Recce party to withdraw.

The following day, the 7th Parachute Battalion and the 2nd Fife and Forfar Yeomanry attacked the village of Wavreille again. The tanks advanced across the open ground, firing as they went, and the paratroopers sprinted from position to position. Casualties were high and we lost five tanks, but the village was captured.

The combination of wintry weather, hilly country and icy roads led to a great deal of grief. No anti-skid devices except chains were available, and these proved to be a mixed blessing, for, while they assisted forward movement, they did not prevent sideways skidding. Damage to guns was also considerable for the ground was frozen hard and the spades could not be dug in, with the result that trail legs were bent and cradles and saddles cracked.

A heavy load was thrown on REME, but their recovery sections did most magnificent work under the arduous conditions. At one time 17 recovery vehicles were deployed on the 30 miles of road between Namur and Marche, the Corps axis. A typical instance of recovery work resulted from a sudden operational demand to move two Churchill bridge-layers from Dinant to Maastricht, a journey of about 100 miles. Owing to the bad conditions, two transporters, four wheeled tractors and two tracked tractors were required for the job, which took four days to accomplish.

On January 3rd, the 53rd Division launched an attack between the river Ourthe and the main road running South East from Marche. Although enemy opposition was fairly slight there were several obstacles to the advance. Numerous mines and booby-traps, together with the bad weather, all proved to be delaying factors. The terrain was difficult, being hilly, and, in places, thickly wooded. The cold was intense, and throughout the battle there was about six inches of snow. Patrolling was dangerous owing to the noise and the difficulty of picking out a stationary and camouflaged enemy before he opened fire. However, that day, the troops advanced between 2,000 and 3,000 yards.

During the attack, Trooper RW Trigg was the wireless operator in the leading tank of a troop of the 144th Royal Armoured Corps, supporting the advance by the 2nd Monmouthshires down the road from Hampteau to Rendeux Bas. A few hundred yards short of the objective the road led through a defile formed by a stream on the left and almost vertical cliffs on the right. At this point a road block was encountered and the infantry was held up. Trooper Trigg moved his tank forward to try to engage the enemy, but immediately got a direct hit which killed the tank commander and the gunner. There was no co-driver, and the driver escaped through the escape hatch, leaving Trigg alone in the tank. It would have been quite natural for him to have tried to escape, but he did nothing of the sort. He worked his way into the driver's compartment, a difficult feat in itself, and, although he had little experience of driving, he put the tank into reverse, and drove it back to safety, thus saving it from further damage. For his initiative and courage he was awarded the MM.

The Germans were suffering from the bitter weather probably more than we were. One prisoner taken about this time said that it had been reported to his Commanding Officer that his men were in a bad condition from hunger and freezing feet. Said he: "If the men's feet are freezing, tell them to kick each other in the stern until they thaw out". Typically Teutonic.

On the 5th January, enemy resistance became even more vigorous, and bitter fighting took place all along the Corps front. The 53rd Division could make no progress at all, and in places had to withdraw. The 6th Airborne Division had many determined counter-attacks put in against them, and some enemy troops got back into Bure. On the American sector, too, little progress was made.

The next day our troops had to withdraw from Bure, and the position of stalemate continued. On the 53rd Division's sector the enemy persisted with his counter-attacks. The continuous fighting was putting a severe strain on the troops, but in spite of the severe conditions all the attacks were repulsed and there were innumerable examples of fortitude.

A company of the 7th Royal Welsh Fusiliers had already had 72 hours of strenuous fighting. On one occasion, after a long day's fighting, a heavy counter-attack was launched against them. CSM L Stiff, ignoring the heavy and accurate fire, moved about encouraging and steadying the troops. Later, when it appeared that the forward platoons were being over-run by considerably superior numbers of the enemy, he rallied survivors from them and positioned them around Company Headquarters. He continued to give a fine example of coolness by standing in a shallow slit trench, with close fighting going on all round, and calmly picked off the Germans with his rifle. The attack was beaten off and the company positions maintained. For his bravery and inspiring example to the troops he was awarded the MM.

On the 7th January, 53rd Division made some progress, and the 4th Welsh Regiment captured Grimbiemont and the high ground to the North East of it. By this advance the enemy were denied the use of the road from Marche to La Roche.

The pressure of the First US Army now increased, Marcourt and Marcouray were both captured, and American troops were within a few thousand yards of the key town of Vielfalm. By the night of the 7th, there were definite signs that the enemy was withdrawing on his Western flank in response to the threat of the thrusts from the North and the South.

The next day's events confirmed that the enemy was withdrawing in earnest on the Corps front, in a Southeasterly direction. The 51st Highland Division now relieved the 53rd Division, and, pushing on, found that the villages of Jemelle, Marloie and Hedree were all clear of enemy troops. The American advance continued, and they were now very near the main road from Houffalize to St Vith, which was the enemy's chief escape route.

The next four days were crucial to the enemy. Provided that he could prevent us from cutting any of his vital routes he could get away with merely loss of face. It seemed clear that Von Runstedt had persuaded his master that a little carpet chewing would be preferable to the loss of an army.

For the next 48 hours the withdrawal continued, and our troops were able to push ahead. Intermittent fighting, snow and ice, together with hidden mines, made rapid progress impossible, but the West bank of the River Ourthe was cleared down to just short of La Roche, and a company of the Royal Ulster Rifles of the 6th Airborne Division reached Nassogne.

Next day, opposition was offered to the advance of the 51st Division at Bande, which was eventually overcome, and at La Roche, where a few well-sited machine-gun posts were encountered and which resisted until nightfall.

After the capture of La Roche, the advance to Hives was a fairly stiff fight. The 7th Battalion, The Black Watch, passed through the 1st Battalion, and reached Hives by eight o'clock that night, having encountered a good deal of spandau and mortar fire on the way. They were opposed by SP guns, which finally withdrew, and Hives was captured.

FIGHTING IN THE SNOW NEAR MARCHE IN THE ARDENNES

That night, the 7th Argylls passed through Hives and made for Beaulieu. They encountered stiff opposition from Tiger tanks and SP guns, which knocked out two tanks of a troop of the 1st Northants Yeomanry, who were supporting the Argylls. Eventually, the enemy were outflanked, and our troops reached their objective with the loss of two officers and thirty-two men.

A party of German infantry, supported by SP guns, had been cut off in the town, and these attacked under cover of darkness in an attempt to escape, but they met with little success and a good number of prisoners was taken.

During the attack on Beaulieu, several Victor targets had been fired, chiefly with the medium artillery, to knock out the Panther tanks, one of which was also accounted for by a SP gun of 241 Anti-tank Battery, RA.

In the area captured by the 154th Brigade, which comprised La Roche, Erneuville, Hives, Beaulieu and Cens, the enemy had left behind considerable quantities of equipment, most of which was in perfect order. Some of the major items were three Panther tanks, seven SP guns, two Staff cars, six Half-tracks, two Volkswagons and an 88mm Gun. 152 Brigade collected, among other equipment, no less than thirteen brand new Half-tracks.

Meanwhile, the enemy's unhurried withdrawal East of Champlon continued, and the important road junction, West of the village, was captured.

The 5th Battalion of The Black Watch was moving South from La Roche to Champlon, acting as advance guard to the remainder of the force. Early in the day they contacted an enemy force supported by Panther tanks. One company was ordered to advance round a flank of this force. This company met a strong party of Huns with two Panther tanks and were counter-attacked just as they themselves were preparing to attack, an awkward situation which led to some confusion. CSM J. Geddes gathered the company together and they managed to beat off the attack. Later, two shells hit the Company Headquarters, and the CSM, in company with many others, was badly wounded. He re-organised the Company Headquarters and supervised the evacuation of the wounded, ignoring his own wounds, and refusing to have them dressed. It was only after he had lost consciousness that he was finally evacuated. For his great part in the action, CSM Geddes received the Military Medal.

On the 51st Division front the enemy decided to put up a fight, and, at the end of the day, our troops were still faced by an enemy post covering the main road from La Roche to Bastogne. The American First Army pushed on steadily towards Houffalize, and further South, the Third US Army had a good day's hunting, and took 1,200 prisoners in the area of Bastogne. By this time, it was estimated that the First and Third US Armies had, between them, taken over 30,000 prisoners since December 16th, when the attack began.

One of the prisoners said that he was sick of fighting and glad to be captured by his 'American Comrades'. Unfortunately, his sentiments could not be accepted, as a letter was found on him which he had written to his family. In it he stated that "he and the German Army were once again on the move to glorious victory". He also boasted of his prowess as a warrior!

Some of the prisoners still had great faith in the German "V" weapons, which they were convinced would win the war for them. But perhaps too much credence could not be given to the story of one of them, who said that the German High Command had now ordered the manufacture of a rubber submarine which would keep on circling round England until the island was erased.

The most important event of the next day was the cutting of the Houffalize — St Vith road by the First US Army, which blocked one of the main enemy escape routes. The 51st Division was still resisted by the 2nd Panzer Division, and it was not until evening that the men of the 1st Gordons were able to fight their way into Nisramont. The 14th January saw the final clearing of the enemy between the River Ourthe and its tributary, the Ourthe Occidentale. Contact was also made with troops of the Third US Army.

The converging attacks of the First and Third US Armies came together on 16th January. There was now no longer any danger of a counter-attack in force; rather was the enemy concerned in salvaging what armoured and motorised elements of the Fifth and the Sixth SS Panzer Armies he could, and, while our fighter bombers could still operate, he was having an unhappy time.

Further, the Russians had now launched their winter offensive, and already it was apparent that the Germans could not hold them with the forces they had available in the East. From now on they would have to be content to defend themselves as best they could on both the East and Western fronts.

Four main factors had been responsible for the defeat of the enemy's bold plan to reach Antwerp. First, the quick appreciation of the situation and the consequent rapid re-grouping of the American and British Corps; secondly, the magnificent resistance of the Allied troops, most especially the heroic stands by the Americans at Bastogne and around Malmedy; thirdly, the break in the weather, which enabled the Allied Air Forces to strike their hardest blows; and, finally, the German shortage of petrol caused by their failure to find the dumps they expected, and by the terrific hammering that the enemy lines of communication received from the air.

30 Corps, pulled from the planning rooms in the North to help stem the unexpected German attack, was now free to return, and, in the middle of January, the Black Boar returned to Boxtel to sharpen his tusks for the next affray.

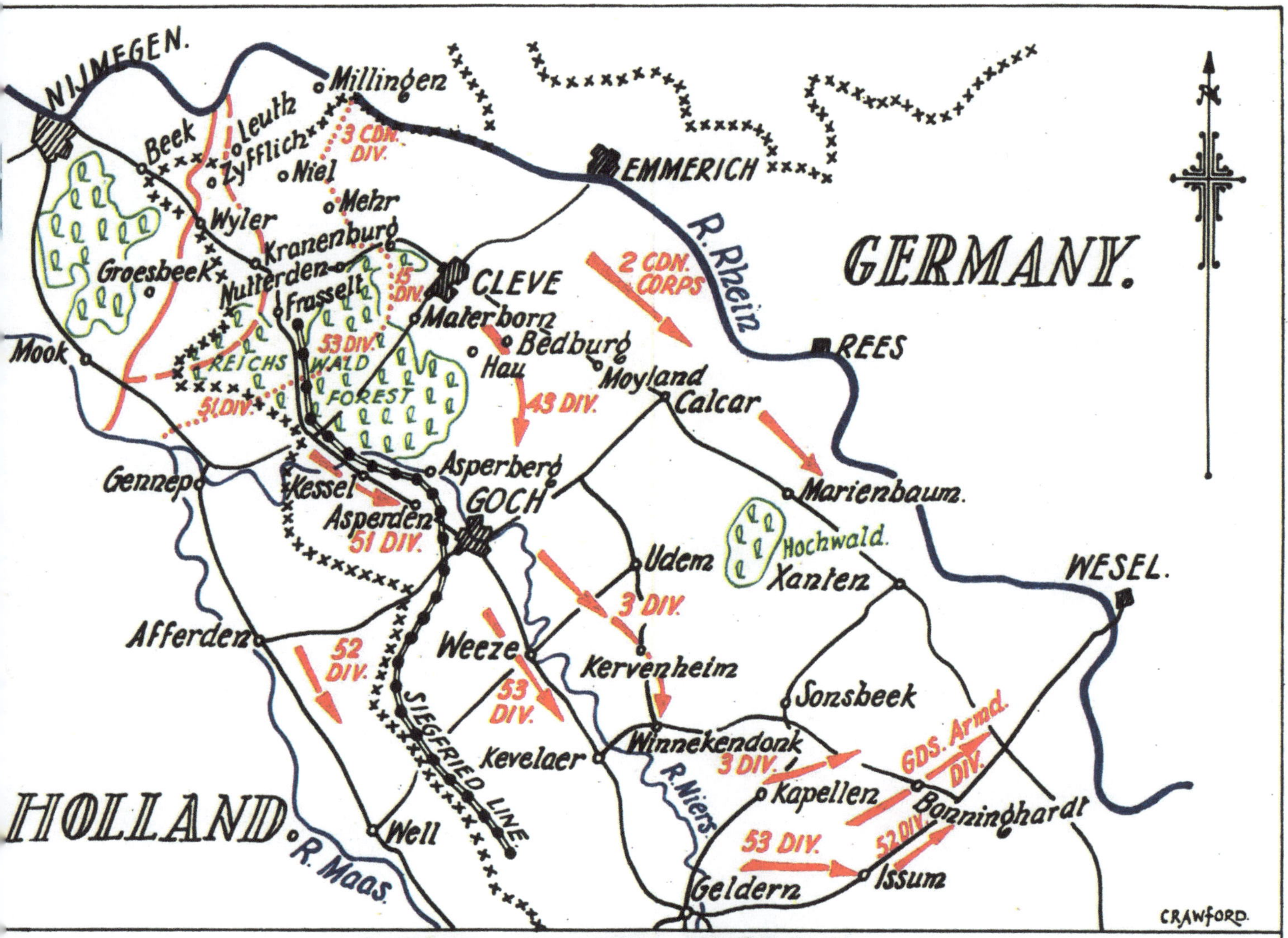

INTO THE RING.

ALLIED LINE AT 10·30 8 FEB.

ALLIED LINE AT MIDNIGHT 8/9 FEB.

ALLIED LINE AT MIDNIGHT 9/10 FEB.

SCALE 1:250,000.

0 5 10

· Miles ·

CHAPTER NIEN

INTO THE RING

Part I

An informal meeting between Field Marshal Montgomery and Lieut. General Horrocks in the Field Marshal's car at Sittard one day that winter can be said to have sealed the fate of the German Armies West of the Rhine. It was then that the Field Marshal unrolled the plan in which 30 Corps was to play the major part, and the foundations for the great operation "Veritable" were laid.

The planning had been interrupted by the German offensive in the Ardennes, but with the turn of the tide in that sector Corps HQ. returned to the task of preparing the operation which was to destroy all the enemy troops between the River Maas and the River Rhine. When this had been done there would remain but "one more river to cross", and then the heart of Germany would be exposed to the final thrust.

30 Corps' first part in the operation was to clear the Reichswald Forest, and the towns of Cleve and Goch to the North and South of it respectively. It was to be no easy task, for strong defence lines lay between us and the Rhine. First there were the firmly held outposts of the Siegfried Line, then the Siegfried Line itself, and finally a fortified lay-back position.

Many towns and villages in this area had been turned into strong-points by the enemy, and although the Siegfried Line was now overgrown, it was anticipated that it contained a certain number of concrete fortifications.

The Reichswald itself was no mean obstacle, consisting as it did of closely growing trees covering an area approximately nine miles long by five miles wide. The forest was divided by numerous rides, but these were narrow and unmetalled, and it was unlikely that they would be suitable for heavy traffic. There were no roads through the Forest from the West to the East, in which direction the attack was to be made.

There was one good road to the North of the Forest running from Nijmegen, through Kranenburg to Cleve, along which the main attack must go, while to the South of it was marshy ground through which flowed the River Niers.

This river runs through Geldern in the South to Goch, and then turns roughly Westwards to join the Maas just above Gennep. Beyond the Reichswald the country was much more open, although commanded by the fortified towns such as Goch, Weeze and Udem. It was realised that here was good going for our tanks, although it was expected that the swampy nature of the ground at the start of the operation would hamper them considerably. But it was hoped that, if all went well, the Guards Armoured Division would be able to make a dash Eastwards, and seize intact the important bridge over the River Rhine at Wesel.

On the left the Canadians were to hold the line of the River Waal, and on our right the Americans were to thrust Northwards across the River Roer and link up with our advance. For this operation 30 Corps came under the command of the First Canadian Army, and under 30 Corps itself was to be arrayed the mightiest concentration of troops ever assembled under one Corps. Our strength was to be over 200,000, and was to consist of one armoured division, six infantry divisions, three armoured brigades, eleven regiments of the 79th Armoured Division, and five Army Groups Royal Artillery.

When planning began snow was on the ground and preparations were made accordingly, but there was always the probability of a thaw, and at the end of January the thaw duly came, causing many last minute alterations. The roads became covered in slush and mud, and transport was once again going to have a heavy time of it. Main roads, so vital for supplies, deteriorated rapidly, while minor roads completely collapsed. It was while conditions were at their worst that troops and vehicles began to concentrate for the forthcoming battle.

During this period the Royal Engineers had the huge task of reconditioning some 400 miles of existing roadway, and constructing 100 miles of new roads.

To reach the Corps concentration area the units had to make long journeys, for three divisions had been left in the Ardennes, and one division and two armoured brigades were in the Geilenkirchen area. It was obvious that, with the limited time available and the urgent necessity for secrecy, the movement would present great difficulties, and need most careful planning. Movement staffs were augmented, and a huge traffic control organisation, consisting of over 1,600 men was set up.

The great move took place, and, miraculously went without a hitch. At the time appointed movement staffs were able to report that this huge assembly of over 200,000 men, with their vehicles, tanks, guns, and ammunition, had been completed.

The Germans had hoped that their abortive offensive in the Ardennes had at any rate prevented us staging any further attacks during the winter. Operation Veritable was to shatter their hopes, and the Corps Commander announced his determination to fight, day and night, unceasingly until the German Army in the North was destroyed. The end was in sight so long as we gave the Hun no rest, and in a Personal Message to his troops Field Marshal Montgomery summed up the situation:

"The operations of the Allies on all fronts have now brought the German war to its final stage. There was a time, some years ago, when it did not seem possible that we could win this war; the present situation is that we cannot lose it: in fact the terrific successes of our Russian Allies on the Eastern front have brought victory in sight.

In 21 Army Group we stand ready for the last round. There are many of us who have fought through the previous rounds; we have won every round on points; we now come to the last and final round, and we want, and will go for, the knock-out blow.

The rules of the last round will be that we continue fighting till the final count; there is no time limit. We know our enemy well; we must expect him to fight hard to stave off defeat, possibly in the vain hope that we may crack before he does. But we shall not crack; we shall see this thing through to the end. The last round may be long and difficult, and the fighting hard; but we now fight on German soil; we have got our opponent where we want him; and he is going to receive the knock-out blow; a somewhat unusual one delivered from more than one direction.

You remember the poem written by a soldier of the Eighth Army in Africa before going into battle, in one verse of which he described what he considered we were fighting for:

"Peace for the kids, our brothers freed,
A kinder world, a cleaner breed".

Let us see to it that we achieve this object, so well expressed by a fighting man of the British Empire.

And so we embark on the final round, in close co-operation with our American Allies on our right, and with complete confidence in the successful outcome of the onslaught being delivered by our Russian Allies on the other side of the ring. Somewhat curious rules, you may say. But the whole match has been most curious; the Germans began this all-out contest and they must not complain when in the last round they are hit from several directions at the same time.

Into the ring, then, let us go. And do not let us relax until the knock-out blow has been delivered. Good luck to you and God bless you.

B. L. Montgomery,
Field Marshal."

The Corps Commander decided to attack with five infantry divisions. The 51st Highland Division on the right was ordered to take the South West corner of the Reichswald, and prevent any enemy movement from the South. The 53rd Welsh Division was to seize the high ground at the North West corner of the Forest, and then move Eastwards. The 15th Scottish Division was to take Kranenburg, and the high ground overlooking Cleve. The 2nd Canadian Division was given the task of capturing Wyler, and the 3rd Canadian Division on the extreme left of the Corps front was to take Zifflich and Leuth. The 43rd Division, and the Guards Armoured Division were to follow on behind the 15th Division, and would be used for exploitation as circumstances allowed.

At five o'clock on the morning of February 8th the big effort to exterminate the German Army began when the greatest artillery barrage in history opened up on the German positions. For five hours machine-guns, bofors, tanks, 17 pounders, heavy Ack Ack, rockets, 25 pounders, 4.5s, 5.5s, and the big gentlemen in the back row all contributed to the ear-splitting pandemonium. Never before had a Corps been supported by such a devastating weight of metal, and during the first day over half a million rounds, weighing some 11,000 tons were fired from over 1,200 guns.

In a letter captured later, a German soldier described his experiences that morning. "When Tommy began his attack", he wrote, "he started with such a terrific artillery barrage that we lost leave of our senses. I shall not forget my experiences in the Reichswald for a long, long time."

The enemy's reply was feeble. It was estimated that there were four battalions of Divisional artillery, and four G. H. Q. units ranged against us, but very few of them fired at all. A prisoner captured later stated that six out of twelve guns in his regiment had been knocked out in our counter-battery programme. Enemy communications were totally disrupted, lines being cut by the barrage, and a prisoner said that the bombardment gave them the impression of an overwhelming force opposed to them, and with no communications at all they felt it was useless to resist.

At 7.40 the bombardment ceased, and a smoke screen was laid down. This lured the enemy into laying down defensive fire, and enabled our Survey Regiment to locate the enemy batteries, which were still active.

In the air too the Corps had terrific support, for, in addition to the whole of the Second Tactical Airforce, the "Heavies" of the 9th U. S. Bombardment Division, and of Bomber Command were available.

At half-past ten the Divisions attacked. Thanks to the tremendous artillery bombardment opposition was slight, for the enemy was numbed, and had lost the power to fight. The barrage moved slowly Eastwards as the assaulting troops and tanks moved forward. So began "Veritable", an operation which was to last for 28 days of fierce day and night fighting. In spite of mines, and the appalling mud, progress was good, by midnight all the day's objectives had been taken, and there were over 1,100 prisoners.

One of the first units to be over-run was the Stomach Batta lion, a collection of duodenal sufferers engaged on preparing defences which they, no doubt, hoped would be manned by others. However, they had been ordered to defend them themselves, but surrendered without putting up much of a fight.

The attack on Kranenburg was made almost unsupported by tanks, as owing to the wet ground they all became bogged. Flail tanks were used to beat a path through suspected minefields, while Sappers undertook the responsibility of clearing the road. The Scottish infantry of the 15th Division were so eager to get on that they trod on the heels of the Sappers, and indeed, eventually passed them. Occasionally a gunner half-track or an infantry anti-tank gun would blow up on a mine. Whenever one of these vehicles blocked the road, a bulldozer would be quickly on the scene to topple it into the ditch, often before the distracted crew had had time to salvage their precious rations, ammunition, and other possessions.

Major I. H. Murray was in command of the right hand forward company of the 10th Battalion the Highland Light Infantry in the assault on Kranenburg. The Company on the left was held up by a minefield, but Major Murray realised that he would have to go on to take advantage of the barrage which was creeping forward according to plan. There were many strong-points in the town, supported by enemy Spandau and Nebelwerfer fire. Murray organised, and in some cases led the assaults on the strong-points personally. Kranenburg was finally cleared, largely due to his initiative and spirited agressiveness. He was awarded the Military Cross.

The area between the Kranenburg road and the Rhine, in which the Canadians were operating, was already flooded, but the

3rd Canadian Division quickly captured Zifflich, making their assault across the water in Buffaloes of the 79th Armoured Division, while Calgary Highlanders of the 2nd Canadian Division stormed into the strong-point of Wyler.

In Zifflich a Crab of B Squadron, 1st Border and Lothian Yeomanry, with Corporal Keenan in charge, flailed its way down the village street in the gathering dusk, firing its guns as it went, and this was quite enough to cause the surrender of its garrison of about 100 Huns. These amphibious operations on the left flank earned for the 3rd Canadian Division the title "Water Rats".

Moving along appalling tracks in the drizzling rain, Welsh infantry of the 53rd Division had broken through the enemy's defensive position, and were well into the Reichswald, supported by tanks of the 34th Armoured Brigade. The Churchill tanks moved along the sides of the forest tracks when they could, crashing through the trees, and preceded on foot by their commanders. They provided powerful support for the infantry with their guns. On this particular sector of the front the Churchills were, in fact, the only tanks to keep up with the infantry, and a wide anti-tank ditch was successfully bridged with the aid of a Churchill bridge-laying tank. The flails and Crocodiles had been bogged down immediately after leaving the start-line.

On the right flank the 51st Highland Division came upon strong opposition. The fighting in the Reichswald was said to be the toughest the Highland Division had had since El Alamein. Veterans who had fought through the desert campaign were agreed that the Hun, on his own soil, was the stiffest proposition they had met. "It was real honest-to-God infantry stuff," a senior officer said, "with no punches barred."

One company, containing many new recruits, had penetrated three-quarters of a mile into the Forest when they came upon a strong German defensive position. Two hundred Germans were lined up along a ride, while three hundred more were in the defences themselves. Badly outnumbered as they were, the young Highlanders dashed in to the attack, and, so determined was their assault, that it was not long before the Germans were utterly routed, and over a hundred and fifty prisoners were taken.

On the left flank the Canadians continued their attacks through the night, and at midnight infantry set off in Buffaloes to attack Niel. The command craft was hit, the infantry commander killed, and the remaining passengers and crew wounded. Lieut J. K. Tarling R. E. took command, and ordered artillery fire on the objective, which not only kept the enemy's heads down, but also enabled the Buffaloes to keep direction. Niel itself was on dry land, and the infantry, assisted by fire from the Buffaloes, had captured it by half past six on the morning of February 9th. On the same night Zandpol was attacked in the same way, and once again an Engineer officer, Captain R. C. A. Cunningham, took charge of the infantry, and led them on to their objective. Later he led them into Leuth.

While Captain Cunningham was in command over 200 prisoners were taken, including one small party of Germans who, having been forewarned of the impending attack, were found waiting to surrender, spick and span in their best uniforms, and cleanly shaven.

Early the next morning, February 9th, the 15th Scottish Division continued their advance. Five attempts had been made during the night to bridge a wide anti-tank ditch which lay across the axis, but only one succeeded. Two battalions were passed over this solitary bridge, and quickly captured Nutterden. During the afternoon the 44th Infantry Brigade occupied the high ground overlooking Cleve.

This historical old town, reputed to be the birthplace of Siegfried, the mythical hero of German legends, lay shattered by the terrific air bombardments to which it had been subjected, and the famous castle and cathedral were both in ruins. The Germans had evacuated civilians from this and other towns in the area.

Meanwhile the men of the 53rd Division, fighting forward grimly without a pause for 36 hours through the dripping forest, reached the high ground South West of Materborn that evening. The experience gained by them in the Ardennes was proving invaluable in this difficult forest battle. On the right flank the 51st Highland Division managed to get astride the main road from Mook to Gennep in two places.

The 43rd Wessex Division was now ordered forward, and that night, (February 9th), the infantry, riding on the tanks of their old friends the 8th Armoured Brigade, travelled along the Kranenburg road towards Cleve. The Germans had blown the Rhine dykes, and the floods were rising fast. From the road to the North was a desolate expanse of water, and the road itself was awash in places. In Kranenburg 190 Field Regiment of the 15th Division reported that their Headquarters was surrounded by water, which was still rising.

Driving on through the night, their path lit only by the flashes of the guns and the few searchlights which were providing artificial moonlight, the 43rd Division turned off the main axis near Nutterden, and made its way by muddy country roads to the South Western outskirts of Cleve. Solitary German bombers were hovering overhead, occasionally dropping a stick of bombs, and German gunners were registering on the road.

The situation in Cleve was obscure, although it was thought that the Germans had withdrawn. In the early morning of the 10th the leading elements of 129 Brigade contacted enemy in the outskirts of the town. Supported by tanks of the Sherwood Rangers Yeomanry, they soon brushed this opposition aside, and Lieutenant Gaiger, commanding a troop of the Ranger's tanks, led them on foot past the bomb craters in the rubble-filled streets at the Southern edge of the town.

As dawn broke enemy S. P. guns and tanks were seen moving in the South Western part of the town, and enemy infantry, whose reveille had been put forward by our early arrival, began scrambling out of cellars and sniping. The men of the 4th Battalion, the Wiltshire Regiment went after them, and a free-for-all ensued amid the craters and the rubble.

The German garrison in Cleve had obviously been taken by surprise. In another part of the town Captain Coleman of the Sherwood Rangers came across a party of German cyclists, who were nonchalantly testing the smooth running of their chains by back-pedalling. A sharp burst of machine-gun fire caused them to change the direction of their pedalling in a hurry.

The enemy soon recovered from his surprise, and put up a stubborn resistance backed by heavy mortar fire. All day confused and heavy fighting continued, in which 129 Brigade Headquarters itself became involved, but it was until the following day, (the 11th), that Cleve was finally cleared of the enemy. During the battle a platoon of the 5th Battalion the Wiltshire Regiment forced the surrender of eight German officers and 170 men, while another enemy party of one officer and 78 men were fought, cornered, and captured by Lieutenant E. A. Mundy M. C., and 20 gunners of the 59th Anti-tank Regiment. In the latter action even the cook, Gunner E. Drinkwater, left the cooking of the men's breakfast to join in the fray.

Meanwhile the only road along which supplies could be brought to the 43rd and 15th Divisions was under water, and only Dukws and Buffaloes could make the journey. As a result of experience gained by the Dutch in 1926 when the Rhine overflowed its banks, it was decided to blow certain dykes North East of Nijmegen. About two million gallons an hour poured through these breaches, but the enemy countered by blowing the dykes on the Alter Rhine, and this let in about the same quantity.

Further, the only axis of the 53rd Division had collapsed, and was closed for repairs, and traffic had to be diverted along the 15th Division axis. A number of the Dukws working on this route missed a turning into the Reichswald, and went nearly into

Cleve before they realised their mistake. They stopped and asked some soldiers where they were, and suddenly found they were speaking to German troops. The surprise and alarm was mutual. However all the Dukws, except one which was ditched, turned round in the minimum of time and returned safely.

Casualties, too, had to be evacuated by Dukws, many of the wounded men still receiving blood transfusion as they were carried away. 129 Field Ambulance of the 43rd Division was at one stage receiving casualties from elements of three divisions, and because of the flooding and the consequent slowness of evacuation, was at one period holding 150 casualties.

It could be seen that the appalling weather and ground conditions would slow down the Corps advance to a serious extent. At one time the only method of getting supplies to the 53rd Division along the forest tracks was by towing the usually dependable Weasels through the mud with Bulldozers.

Now the enemy was calling upon his reserves, and the well-known fighting men of his tough parachute divisions were identified in the battle for Cleve.

In the South the Highlanders were pressing forward to take Gennep from the North, and to clear the Mook—Goch road, and so provide another urgently needed supply route.

A troop of armoured cars of the Derbyshire Yeomanry, (51st Reconnaissance Regiment), ran into an ambush in the village of Zelderheide, and all the crews were killed except the troop commander, Lieutenant D. Partridge who was wounded, and Sergeant Brown who managed to bail out with two other men. The Lieutenant was captured, but Sergeant Brown found shelter in a small chicken house, while his friends hid nearby. There they remained until it was dark, and the Boche dug slit trenches close by, quite unaware of their presence. That night they managed to return to their own lines, and a little later Lieutenant Partridge was rescued when a Battalion of the Black Watch over-ran the German dressing station to which he had been taken.

During the night of 10th/11th February the Highland Division made a silent crossing of the River Niers, and by early morning had established a small bridgehead on the isthmus between the Niers and the Maas. Gennep was then assaulted from the rear, and the German paratroopers who were holding the town were taken by surprise.

They quickly recovered, and put up a fierce resistance, firing from windows, cellars and rooftops. Gradually the Highlanders fought their way in, the Germans making desperate efforts to beat them back. It was another rough-and-tumble for the Highlanders, who entered into it with zest, and within 24 hours the town was in our hands.

During the street fighting in the town, a Company commander of the 5th Battalion, the Black Watch, was killed, and Lieutenant D. Crockett, a platoon commander, took over his company. They were held up by a strong-point in the railway station, and the Lieutenant personally directed flamethrowing tanks on to the target under heavy fire. He then led his company in a spirited charge, and completely routed the enemy. They dealt similarly with another strong-point in a factory, and once again overcame the enemy resistance. Lieutenant Crockett, whose gallantry was an inspiration to his men, was awarded the Military Cross.

About this time a most unusual, but nevertheless welcome event took place South of Cleve. In the early morning a strong force of paratroopers was seen forming up for an attack. Then, however, to everyone's amazement, instead of attacking, they surrendered en masse. Five officers, including the Battalion Commander, and 174 other ranks gave themselves up without a shot being fired.

Meanwhile the dams at Duren, referred to in a previous chapter, had been blown by the enemy, and the Roer valley was flooded. This would prevent any American advance across the river until the waters had gone down, which would take at least a week. Hence the enemy were able to withdraw the reserves from that area, and use them against 30 Corps. The 15th Panzer, the 116th Panzer and the Panzer Lehr Division were all identified on the Corps Front. A series of determined counter attacks were put in by the enemy, and very bitter fighting followed. The full might of the Corps Artillery was released, and this, together with the determined defence of the leading infantry, and the flights of rocket-firing Typhoons which were always hovering over the battlefield ready to pounce, succeeded in breaking up all assaults.

The Commander of the 43rd Division now decided to clear the enemy from the village of Materborn, South West of Cleve, where they were strongly ensconced. The 5th Battalion, the Duke of Cornwall's Light Infantry, were ordered to attack Materborn, while the 7th Battalion, the Somerset Light Infantry, were to pass through to clear as far as Hau, which lies on the main Cleve—Goch road.

The Cornishmen cleared Materborn, and the Somersets passed through them, but became engaged in a brisk fight with enemy Spandau teams and S. P. guns at the crossroads between Materborn and Hau, which soon became known as "Tiger Corner". Fighting continued throughout the night in bitter weather conditions, by the light of burning tanks. Snow lay in the stiff gas-capes which the men were wearing as water-proofs, and the Bren gunners, who had to be changed at frequent intervals, found it necessary to use two fingers to pull their triggers, but by the morning Hau was captured.

During the house-clearing operations Sergeant Major Evans of the 7th Battalion the Somerset Light Infantry approached an isolated farmhouse from which a chink of light was showing, with the Company runner, Private Hough. With a grenade in one hand, and his rifle tucked under his arm, the Sergeant Major entered, and found twelve Germans asleep in one room. Seeing them asleep he put the grenade in his pocket, and fired a shot through the ceiling. It was a piece of chivalry which nearly proved disastrous, for at the noise of the shot a German officer appeared from another room, and he and the Sergeant fired together. The officer fell, but now the others started to move, and another Hun made a rush from the back of the house. It was an ugly moment, and the Sergeant Major ordered Hough to fetch a Bren team. Fortunately at this moment Major Durie arrived with a Bren gunner, Private Bond. A burst was fired into the room, and that was enough for the inmates. One of them, who spoke English, called out that they surrendered.

On February 12th a troop of B Squadron the 43rd Reconnaissance Regiment attempted to move down the road from Hau to Goch. When the four armoured cars entered the village of Niederdam everything was suspiciously quiet. Quite suddenly Germans sprang up from ditches and slit-trenches, and a pitched battle began. The second and fourth cars were hit, and caught fire, but some of the crews managed to get out, riding on the back of the leading car, which quickly turned round.

Lieutenant Joslin the troop commander, was withdrawing from the ambush, when he saw a German half-track pull out into a side-track. He hit it twice with shells from his 37 mm gun, and had the satisfaction of seeing it burst into flames. As he pulled back a startled German officer ran out of the village cafe. He had obviously been disturbed at his breakfast, for he held a plate of ham and eggs in his hand. A sharp burst of machine-gun fire persuaded him that it was safer inside the house, and the remainder of the troop withdrew to safety.

The Canadians now took over the responsibility for Cleve, and a brigade group of the 15th Scottish Division pushed on towards Calcar. The 7th Battalion of the Seaforths who were mounted on Kangaroos, and supported by a squadron of Churchill tanks of the 4th Coldstream Guards, soon ran into trouble. The enemy had the road well covered with his artillery and mortars, and, as the Churchills and Kangaroos were unable to get off the road owing to ditches and the soft ground, many of them were hit, and the road was soon dotted with burning vehicles. It appeared that the advance was held up, but the Seaforths dismounted, and, going forward entirely unsupported by tanks, reached the village of Hasselt by dark.

In the Reichswald Forest, the 53rd Welsh Division had to bear the brunt of the counter-attacks made by our old enemies the 15th Panzer Grenadier Division. The Germans were well supported by SP guns which shot down the rides, and they fought strongly, but the Welshmen yielded no ground.

Further South, the Highland Division made good progress, and captured the important cross-roads at Hekkens. The attack on the cross-roads was made by the 154th Brigade with the support of no less than four field regiments, nine medium regiments and six heavy batteries. After stiff fighting, the opposition was overcome and 160 prisoners taken. The capture of the cross-roads opened up a vital axis for the whole army. The Corps Commander told Brigadier Oliver that this capture and the later capture of Kessel had a determining effect on the course of the whole of operation "Veritable" by making possible the use of the Southern axis.

It now became clear that the German Army was determined to fight it out on the West of the Rhine, which was what we had hoped for, but hardly expected. We were ready to seize this opportunity. From now on, our success need not be assessed in ground gained, but rather in the number of German dead and prisoners.

Part II

Now began the attack which, in the Corps Commander's opinion, was the turning point of Operation Veritable. The 43rd Division broke out of Cleve and drove Southward, in the face of fierce opposition, to seize the escarpment overlooking Goch from the North East. It by-passed the strongly held Cleve Forest, a carefully co-ordinated fire plan keeping the enemy in this wood innocuous during the advance. The plan throughout was to seize Goch by securing the high ground of the escarpment and thus unhinge the entire lay-back defensive system north of the town. Opposition was extremely bitter. Groups of farm buildings had been turned into carefully prepared strongpoints. They had to be taken one by one against Panzer and Panzer Grenadier units and a Battalion of Van der Heydte's paratroop-saboteurs of Ardennes fame.

The 4th Battalion, the Dorset Regiment, led the break-out on the morning of February 15th, and soon became involved in very

MEN OF THE 15TH SCOTTISH DIVISION IN KRANENBURG SHORTLY AFTER ITS CAPTURE

severe fighting. With the 7th Battalion the Hampshire Regiment on the right, and the 5th Battalion the Dorset Regiment on the left, it was hoped to clear a start line for the further advance of 214th Brigade. The weather was foggy and the roads were very bad, and it was not until next morning that, at the point of the bayonet, the start line was cleared.

Then the 7th Battalion the Somerset Light Infantry and the 1st Battalion the Worcestershire Regiment passed through and made headway in spite of the severe opposition. That night, aided by searchlights, the armoured column of the 5th Duke of Cornwall's Light Infantry, supported by a squadron of the 4th/7th Dragoon Guards, dashed Southwards. This was the same armoured column that had made the spectacular dash to the Neder Rijn during the plunge into Holland. Next day the 4th Battalion the Somerset Light Infantry put in a further attack, and, later that day, 214th Brigade was firmly ensconced on the escarpment overlooking Goch.

Goch, an important road and rail centre, lay in ruins. Since the break-out from Cleve, the 43rd Division had advanced ten miles and had taken 2,300 prisoners. They had overcome a series of fierce counter-attacks by some of the best German troops, and they had secured the feature which opened the way into Goch.

Meanwhile, the 15th Scottish Division was continuing its drive towards Calcar, and the Glasgow Highlanders were planning an attack on the village of Moyland and Moyland Wood, which was known to be a strong enemy gun area. A Commando officer, who had obtained 48 hours leave for the occasion, joined the Highlanders. He had a personal interest in the attack for his name was Lieutenant van Moyland, and he was none other than the grandson of the owner of Schloss Moyland, the castle which dominated the village.

He knew the ground like the palm of his hand, and his knowledge of the moat and the bridges, the walls and the grounds, was of the greatest assistance. He was not perturbed when he heard that Typhoons were to attack the Schloss, his one anxiety being that the Huns would remove his sporting guns before he got there. Unfortunately, his leave expired before the attack went in, and, as the Canadians took over this sector from the Scottish Brigade, the Glasgow Highlanders never carried out this assault.

By now the 53rd Division had cleared the Reichswald and had left the forest gloom to approach the town of Goch. A Battalion Commander of this Division, described the clearing of the Reichswald, said: "It was Spandau versus Bren the whole way through".

On the night of February 16th, a company of the 1st Battalion, the Oxfordshire and Buckinghamshire Light Infantry, was ordered to seize some high ground near Asperberg. The assault was made behind a creeping barrage across 400 yards of open ground, and was carried out with great dash and determination in the face of very heavy fire. The assaulting platoon gained the high ground and went on to clear some farm buildings in the vicinity. There followed a great deal of confused fighting, and, on one occasion, the platoon commander, Lieutenant A. F. M. Paget, himself killed nine Germans, each armed with a Spandau, who counter-attacked them. First light found our men firmly on the high ground, with 16 prisoners, and 34 enemy dead around their positions.

Lieutenant Paget, who was the son of General Paget, showed great initiative and bravery during the whole of this action, and he was awarded the D. S. O.

Meanwhile, The Highland Division, with the 32nd Guards Brigade under command, was approaching Goch from the West. The 154th Brigade made a grand crossing of the River Niers in front of the town of Kessel. The 7th Battalion of The Black Watch secured a bridge-head over a loop of the river, after which the 1st Battalion, The Black Watch, passed through them and widened the bridgehead, just West of Kessel. Then, on the following night, the 7th Battalion, The Argyll and Sutherland Highlanders, were passed through to capture Kessel. Everything went according to plan, and Kessel was taken. In this action, which finally secured the vital route via the Hekkens cross-roads, four hundred prisoners were captured. The crossing of the River Niers, was, of necessity, very hastily laid on, and it was the first time that any of the troops taking part had used Buffaloes. This successful operation was one of the hardest battles that the 154th Brigade was involved in during operation "Veritable". Very shortly afterwards, a Class 40 bridge was laid down over the river at Kessel.

The 152nd Brigade went on and captured the village of Asperden, on the 16th of February, thus breaching a portion of the Siegfried Line and opening the way into Goch.

The attack on Goch began in earnest on February 18th when the 44th Infantry Brigade of the 15th Scottish Division attacked from the North supported by a heavy artillery programme. Royal Engineers of the 43rd Division, working silently under the noses of the enemy, had constructed six tank crossings over a 20 feet deep anti-tank ditch during the previous night.

The 53rd Division was ordered to clear the Eastern bank of the River Niers, while 51st Highland Division attacked the town from the South East. The 153rd and the 154th Brigades had a stiff fight clearing the town. The 5th Battalion, The Black Watch, made a highly successful attack to the South, just short of the woods, and, in spite of heavy casualties, cleared the area of the enemy.

The German parachutists fought tenaciously among the rubble of the ruined town, and it was not until the evening of the 21st that Goch was in our hands. Flame throwing tanks of the 79th Armoured Division once again proved their extreme value in street fighting, and obstinate pockets of resistance were frequently burned out by their use.

Over 800 prisoners were taken, including the German Garrison Commander and his staff, and, by this time, the total number captured by the Corps in Operation Veritable exceeded 10,000.

The 15th Scottish Division carried on the advance to the South East, towards the town of Weeze. The 43rd Division was now withdrawn to rest and refit in the Cleve area, and, subsequently, came under the command of the Second Canadian Corps.

Meanwhile, the 52nd Lowland Division and the 3rd British Division had come under the command of 30 Corps. The 52nd Division took over the right flank from the Highland Division, while the 3rd British Division approached Weeze from the North West.

On the 23rd of February the Roer floods had subsided sufficiently to enable the 9th U. S. Army to start its big offensive across the river, and bridgeheads were quickly established between Linnich and Duren. Thanks to the withdrawal of the enemy's reserves to face the onslaught of 30 Corps, the opposition was weakened and the Americans advanced rapidly. Almost unopposed, the American armour rolled East and North, and Roermond, Erkelenz and Munchen Gladbach were taken after only a few days fighting.

On the same day, Lieut. General B. G. Horrocks issued a personal message to his troops:

> "You have now successfully completed the first part of your task. You have taken approximately 12,000 prisoners and killed large numbers of Germans. You have broken through the Siegfried Line and drawn on to yourselves the bulk of the German reserves in the West. A strong U. S. offensive was launched over the Roer at 0330 hours this morning against positions which, thanks to your efforts, are lightly held by the Germans. Our offensive has made the situation most favourable for our Allies and greatly increased their prospects of success. Thank you for what you have done so well. If we continue our efforts for a few more days, the German front is bound to crack".

Weeze, the next town to be taken in our drive to the South, was held by the German 8th Parachute Division. The 53rd

Division was to make a frontal attack on the town, but, before it could do so, it was necessary to clear a small ridge to the East of the River Niers which dominated the approaches to the town. The Corps Commander gave this task to the 3rd British Division which had relieved the 15th Scottish. This Division ran into fierce opposition from the determined Paratroopers but finally succeeded in clearing the East bank. Early on the morning of the 24th the 53rd Division attacked, supported by the Flails and Crocodiles of the 79th Armoured Division, and by 400 guns of the Corps artillery. The resistance met was as fierce as any during the whole operation, and the attack was slowed down. Enemy artillery was active and accurate and there was clearly no shortage of ammunition. Eventually, as the Corps artillery was needed to support the Canadians in an operation in the North, the Corps Commander decided to call a halt to the attack on Weeze for the time being.

The Canadian operation was designed to break through the Hochwald "Lay-back" position and to exploit towards Xanten and Wesel, and it began on February 26th. Calcar and Udem were captured and the Hochwald line pierced, but the stubborn resistance of the enemy held the Canadians up there.

The 3rd Division continued to advance, however, and on February 27th the 2nd Battalion the East Yorkshire Regiment captured an important road bridge between Weeze and Udem. The Company, which had overwhelmed the German defenders, found that the enemy had intended to blow the bridge with two 500 lb. bombs, but it was still intact and perfectly sound. The company prepared defensive positions around a nearby house, and very soon paratroopers, a battalion strong, began to counter attack. There was fierce fighting, but the outnumbered Yorkshiremen hung on, and succeeded in keeping the enemy from the bridge.

At one stage in the battle a German tank drove up to the house, and a German officer shouted in excellent English: „Are you all right in there, Tommy?" Finding that Tommy apparently was all right, he pulled back, and fired into the house at point blank range.

Ammunition was running short by this time, and the Germans evidently thought they had wiped out the little British force. Seven of them entered the house, and all were killed. Major R Rutherford MC said that the Germans played cowboys and Indians round the house.

Major "Banger" King won a bar to his DSO in this action by dashing through a hail of fire to the beleagured company with ammunition in a Bren Carrier. Tank support was not available, but artillery armoured OP tanks rose to the occasion, and engaged the enemy. When the battle was over, and the company had been relieved, over 83 dead Germans were counted in the area.

MEN OF THE 51ST HIGHLAND DIVISION WAITING FOR THE START OF THE RHINE CROSSING

The attack on Weeze was resumed on March 1st. The men of the German 22nd Parachute Regiment fought fanatically and flame-throwers were again employed to burn out the nests of the obstinate Huns, and it was not until the following day that the town could be reported clear.

On the same day, the 3rd Division, continuing their advance, reached the town of Kurvenheim, and found it strongly held. The town was an important road centre between Udem and Winnekendonk, (known to our men as "Winnie can stonk"). Men of the 2nd Battalion, the King's Shropshire Light Infantry, had to advance along a partially made road. The banks gave them some cover from enemy fire, but at one point they had to double across a 70 yard gap, swept by a hail of bullets. During part of the battle a white goat followed the Battalion into action.

The leading platoon was pinned down during the attack by heavy fire, and Private Stokes, armed only with a rifle, dashed forward against a hail of bullets, and although he was wounded, captured single handed a farm building, and twelve prisoners. The platoon advanced but again came under heavy fire. Once more Stokes dashed forward, receiving more wounds, but again silencing the enemy. He refused to leave his comrades, and later, while forming up to attack the final objective, the platoon was subjected to intense enemy fire. Although severely wounded and suffering from loss of blood, Stokes advanced again, firing from the hip, but 20 yards from the objective he was swept by a hail of bullets, and fell mortally wounded. As his platoon dashed past him in the final charge, he raised his arm, and shouted, "Goodbye". For his magnificent courage he was awarded a posthumous VC.

The Royal Norfolk Regiment called their part in this operation the Battle of the Billiard Table. They had no time to recce the start line, and found themselves on a flat stretch of ground which they had to cross to reach Kurvenheim. "From the enemy's point of view, it was an ideal killing ground", said a company commander, "There was 800 yards of ground, swept by enemy fire". But in spite of the intense fire, the Norfolks crossed it and gained their objective.

An armoured column consisting of infantry of the Welsh Division and the 8th Armoured Brigade pushed on down the road towards Kevelaer, with tanks of the Reconnaissance Troop of the 4th/7th Dragoon Guards in the lead. The advance was slowed up by felled trees and craters and the tanks were continually forced to make detours. The craters, made by the enemy with 500 lb bombs, were sometimes as much as 70 feet in diameter and 12 feet deep. As they became filled with water faster than they could be pumped out, it became necessary to bridge them, and, in fact, during Operation Veritable, the Royal Engineers had to construct no less than 95 bridges over these obstacles.

The sides of the road were heavily wooded, and all went well until the leading tank left the cover of the trees. Then it was fired on by an anti-tank gun, manned, it was afterwards discovered, by a party of Volksturm. The tank was not hit, and the gunner, Trooper Radcliffe, was about to engage the target when, with a flash and a dull explosion, the tank was disabled by a mine. The driver, Trooper France, was wounded in the legs, and was extricated from the burning tank with great difficulty by the rest of the crew, who were under heavy Spandau fire. The supporting artillery, the 147th Field Regiment, quickly dealt with the anti-tank gun, the mines were cleared by a detachment of Royal Engineers, and the Welsh Division continued its advance towards Kevelaer.

The 1st Battalion of the Oxfordshire and Buckinghamshire Light Infantry, with "A" Squadron of the 4th/7th Dragoon Guards, led the way into Kevelaer. On Saturday, March 3rd, "C" Squadron, with "B" Company of the 12th King's Royal Rifles, linked up at Geldern with the Americans who had been moving up from the South. Thus was completed the encirclement of large numbers of the enemy.

Encountering ever-decreasing opposition, the 52nd Lowland Division, with the 1st Commando Brigade under command, were pushing on down the Eastern bank of the River Maas, while on the left of the Corps front the 3rd British Division had reached Winnekendonk. The 2nd Lincolns went in to attack Winnekendonk, assaulting straight down the main road, instead of using the flanks, which offered better cover. This move certainly surprised the Germans, and after crossing 1,000 yards of open ground under heavy machine gun and mortar fire, the battalion became engaged in fierce street battles. In the incredibly short time of an hour and a quarter the town was taken with 200 prisoners. The Guards Armoured Division, passing through the infantry, pushed on towards Boninghardt, but the cratered roads and blown bridges caused much delay. There was still spirited resistance and heavy fire, and it was not until March 6th that Boninghardt was captured.

It was now quite clear to the enemy that he had lost the battle West of the Rhine, and his main concern now was to evacuate as much of his armour and as many of his troops as he could to the East bank of the Rhine. To accomplish this he concentrated on holding a small bridgehead at Wesel, and it became the urgent task of 30 Corps to reduce this bridgehead as quickly as possible.

Unfortunately, the weather once again favoured the enemy, and did not allow our air forces to exploit their supremacy on what would have been a glorious target. Flying had been badly affected by the weather the whole time, and, in particular, it had not been possible to take many air photographs during the battle. However, the whole area had been well photographed just before the operation began and full use was made of these photographs both before, and during, the battle. Enemy positions had been accurately spotted, and counter-battery programmes were based chiefly on the information obtained from them. The distribution of air photographs, was, in fact, the largest ever made, and 354,000 of them were used by the British troops alone.

In the South the American break-through was complete, and the 1st U. S. Army celebrated the close of nine months fighting in Europe by the capture, on March 6th, of Cologne. On March 7th an armoured column of the same Army captured the railway bridge over the Rhine at Remagen intact, and quickly established a strong bridgehead on the East bank.

On the Corps front on March 8th the liquidation of the Wesel bridgehead was in sight. The Canadians were battering at the gates of Xanten and the enemy's perimeter was being rapidly compressed. That evening, 30 Corps' part in the destruction of the German Army West of the Rhine came to an end, and operational command of all its troops passed to the Second Canadian Corps.

Once again we had done what we had set out to do, and the Boar had wrought great havoc among the rapidly diminishing German forces.

Carefully prepared defensive positions had been penetrated and overcome. Four infantry divisions, three panzer divisions and four parachute divisions had been utterly routed. Nearly 17,000 prisoners had been taken and it was estimated that we had inflicted no fewer than 7,000 casualties, and, now, the springboard to the heart of Germany was in our hands.

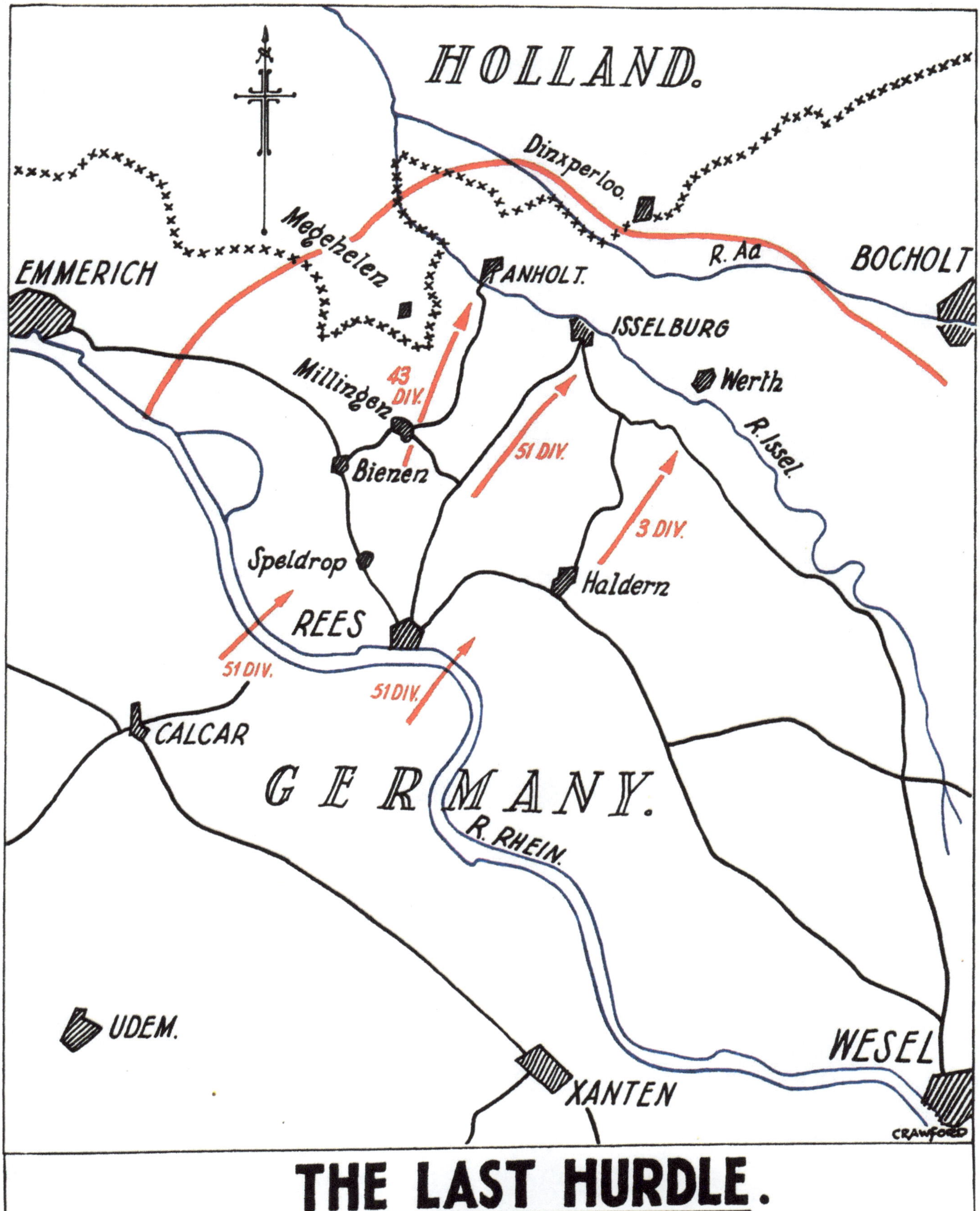

THE LAST HURDLE.

SCALE 1: 110,000.

APPROX. LINE AT 29 MAR. 45.

1 0 1 2 3 4 5

Miles

CHAPTER TEN

THE LAST HURDLE

Many years ago the first recorded crossing of the Rhine was made by Julius Caesar. He tackled the job in the year 55 B. C. and having decided that the best way to get across would be by means of a bridge, he constructed, in ten days, a quite elaborate affair which proved strong enough to take the weight of his army, which passed over in safety. The Sicambri, who were inhabiting the land West of the Rhine at that time, took instant alarm at this incursion, and immediately abandoned the country, fleeing into the forests with all their possessions.

With a view to making the present inhabitants do the same, the Allies now prepared to tackle the crossing of the river, but with rather more elaborate machinery.

The British Second Army now consisted of the 2nd Canadian Corps, and the 8th, 12th and 30th British Corps. It was to make the crossing on a two Corps front between Wesel and Emmerich, with 12 Corps on the right and 30 Corps on the left; and 30 Corps Commander intended to capture Rees and Haldern, establishing a bridgehead preparatory to a further advance into the German Reich.

The assault crossing and the subsequent advance was given the title of Operation Plunder, and, to give a larger picture of the plan, the ultimate aim was to link up, somewhere about the River Elbe, with the Russians, who would start their all-out attack on Berlin a few days after we began.

On the right of the Second Army was the Ninth US Army, and, on the left, the First Canadian Army. 30 Corps itself, reduced in numbers but not in spirit, now had under command the Guards Armoured Division, the 43rd Division, the 51st Highland Division, the 3rd British Division, the 8th Armoured Brigade, and elements of the 79th Armoured Division.

As far back as January, General Dempsey, the Second Army Commander, had made his plans for the crossing of the Rhine. There were some intricate problems to be worked out, and he entrusted the 79th Armoured Division with the task of evolving a suitable technique to overcome the various difficulties. For this purpose the Division set up special Training Wings which thrashed out in theory and then in practice all the problems that presented themselves, and, by March 21st, all personnel were fully trained and ready for the assault.

Meanwhile, the 51st Division, which was to make the assault, had been practising intensive amphibious operations on the River Maas, near Roermond, and they, too, were now fully trained.

For the Royal Engineers this crossing of the Rhine was to be their greatest operation. More sappers came under command of the Chief Engineer, 30 Corps, than at any previous time, a total of 8,000 being employed.

There was not a great deal of time for planning and for marshalling the thousands of tons of equipment into the jumping-off places on the West bank. Further, all movement had to take place at night, but the great task was successfully accomplished under cover of a continuous smoke screen along the Corps front, and the right material was delivered to the right site at the right time.

The task of the Armoured Engineers with 30 Corps in the Rhine crossing was only one of about ten Engineer tasks, but it was in some ways unique. The 5th Assault Regiment, Royal Engineers, had to build and operate four 60 ton ferries to carry tanks across in the early stages. The Rhine was the widest river that had yet been tackled, being some 1,500 feet across, and many modifications were necessary to fit the standard equipment to this particular task, and Major WS Tyzack of the Royal Engineers carried out hasty trials on the River Waal at Nijmegen.

The RAF winches used to operate the rafts occupied many sappers who were wanted for other jobs. Hesitant enquiries were put to the RAF for a few volunteer helpers. It was felt rather hard to ask a RAF balloon-winch operator to exchange his normal seat, out in the blue, for one on the bank of the Rhine in which the enemy might have an intense and unfriendly interest. But 159th Wing, RAF, produced the necessary 50 operators under command of Warrant Officer C Campbell from 150 miles away in twelve hours, and they said they had another 300 volunteers standing by for further vacancies.

The "Combined Operations" aspect was complete when a Royal Naval party under 'Bosun' Lascombe was placed under command to erect an anti-submarine boom downstream from the rafting sites.

Buffaloes, Armoured Bulldozers, RAF winches, Armoured Sledges, 6 ton Matador Lorries borrowed from the gunners, RASC 3-tonners, AVREs and 50 foot pontoon trailers all formed part of the enormous procession that set out on the night of March 21st, without lights, to travel the thirty miles to the concentration area. A Canadian who watched the convoy move slowly past was heard to say: "Gee! Now I've seen everything!"

All the equipment had to be made up into sledge or trailer loads in the concentration area, suitable for tanks to tow forward to the river. An American Camouflage Platoon supervised the camouflaging of the tanks and equipment at first light, and some enterprising Press photographers took pictures of the pontoons, which eventually appeared in the illustrated weeklies as "Royal Naval Landing Craft waiting to move forward for launching into the Rhine".

The towns in the Reichswald area, shattered as they were, harboured vast quantities of troops and equipment during the build-up period. Enemy long-range guns were active and caused a few casualties in the crowded towns. All the Corps artillery had to be brought up under cover of darkness and placed into position by night as these positions were visible from the far bank.

Operation Plunder began on the evening of March 23rd when, between five and six o'clock, medium bombers attacked enemy positions and troops. Then, at six o'clock, the huge artillery programme began.

The terrific fire-power was provided by no less than seventeen Field Regiments, ten Medium Regiments, two Heavy Regiments and two Super-heavy Batteries, supported by innumerable ack-ack and anti-tank guns. The bombardment was designed first to destroy the enemy batteries, and later, increasing in intensity, to neutralise the enemy infantry. An avalanche of metal and streams of tracer poured across the river and continued unabated until the assault crossing went in, when the barrage lifted to targets further inland.

At nine o'clock, in the hazy darkness, the leading Buffaloes of the 30th Armoured Brigade, carrying infantry of the 153rd and 154th Brigades, of the Highland Division, slid into the Rhine. While waiting for their transport, the Highlanders had been singing such songs as 'Loch Lomond', and 'I belong to Glasgow'. Spirits were high.

After a four minute journey the Eastern bank of the Rhine was reached, and Colonel Jolly planted the Royal Tank Regimental flag from Bovington there. The leading waves of Buffaloes carried only men and equipment, but these were quickly followed by others loaded with guns and vehicles.

It was essential to establish line communication as early as possible between the assaulting troops and their Divisional Headquarters. Major Henderson, of the Royal Corps of Signals, followed closely on the tail of the assaulting Buffaloes to establish the necessary communications. The Dukw in which he and his detachment were making the crossing came under heavy fire, and, about twenty yards from the West bank, the Dukw was holed and began to sink. By swimming and clinging on to the cable that they had been towing the men were able to get back to the West bank. The driver, who had been injured, was pinned by the steering wheel, and Major Henderson liberated him and dragged him back to safety.

Wet as they were, Henderson and his men crossed the river in another Dukw. The East bank proved to be too steep to allow the beaching of the Dukw and he swam ashore against a strong current and moored it. He supervised the laying of field cables to each Brigade Headquarters under heavy fire, and for several hours patrolled the lines, personally repairing the breaks that were continually being caused both by the passage of Buffaloes and by shellfire. Major Henderson received the DSO for his part in the operation.

The Dukws, after preliminary trouble getting into and out of the river, continued to ferry the vital ammunition, petrol and supplies across. They found the actual crossing, although longer, comparatively easy, as owing to the greater width the current was not so strong as it had been at Nijmegen and Arnhem.

On our right flank 12 Corps had also put in their assault, and at half past nine a force of 500 heavy bombers dropped high explosives on the town of Wesel. Men of the 1st Commando Brigade were already across, and, by eleven o'clock, 1,200 men with guns and vehicles were on the far side.

On our own front more battalions of the 51st Highland Division followed up the initial landing during the night. Opposition to our assault was not as heavy at first as had been expected, but it soon stiffened and the Highlanders became engaged in bitter fighting in the outskirts of Rees.

Pushing inland West of Rees during the night, men of the 1st Battalion the Black Watch captured the village of Speldrop in the early hours of the next morning. When daylight came the enemy counter-attacked the village with infantry and SP guns, and the fighting became very confused. Lieutenant JR Henderson, appreciating that the holding of the village was vital to the development of the Rhine bridgehead, as it lay astride the main Rees-Emmerich road, volunteered to lead a patrol to find out the extent of the enemy penetration.

The patrol came under intense machine-gun fire and casualties were heavy. Henderson ordered his men to get under cover while he and a Bren gunner went forward alone. Almost immediately the Bren gunner was killed and the officer's revolver was shot from his hand. Using his shovel as a weapon, Lieutenant Henderson charged the machine-gun position and killed the gunner.

He made his way back to his patrol and rushed his men into the only building in the vicinity, although it was already in flames. They had no light automatic weapon, so Henderson crawled back, under heavy fire, to where the Bren gunner had been killed, collected the Bren gun, and made the difficult journey back to his men.

Armed with this weapon the beleagured patrol held out for over twelve hours against all attempts to dislodge them.

During the whole of this time the enemy's attacks were supported by Bazookas fired at short range. For his magnificent gallantry and leadership, Lieutenant Henderson was awarded the DSO.

Until class 40 bridges could be built the only means of getting tanks across the river was by rafts. The 5th Assault Regiment of the Royal Engineers, previously mentioned, moved down to the bank of the river shortly after the assault went in and began to prepare for rafting operations. By dawn on March 24th the first raft was ready and shortly afterwards another one was completed. The two remaining rafts were delayed owing to their site being under intense fire from Rees.

However, by evening, all four rafts were operating successfully. Anxious officers bombarded the raft controlling officers with requests to let their particular tanks go next, but "Bank Control", organised by men of the Royals, was in command and only their word was accepted for priorities.

Accidents and delays were inevitable, and the rafts were frequently in need of repair. One was shot up from the air, and sank, but a replacement was made in four hours. On one occasion a raft was ferrying two Sherman tanks across at once. This, while theoretically possible, was unwise, owing to the patched state of the raft where it had been hit by shell and mortar splinters. The patches gave way and the raft, with its crews and load, sank in twelve feet of water to the accompaniment of many well chosen words from the crews. 350 tanks and SP guns were ferried across in the first 72 hours.

Amphibious tanks of the Staffordshire Yeomanry, in spite of heavy enemy shellfire and difficulties encountered in the river mud, succeeded in landing to support the leading infantry brigades.

Of the many stirring messages that were coming back over the wireless one of the more startling ones was received by the

Adjutant of the 128th Highland Field Regiment, RA. It read simple: "CO now drunk". Things were not so bad as they seemed, however, for it was actually a code message meaning that the Commanding Officer, Lieut Colonel JEL Morris, DSO, had crossed the Rhine and was safely established on the far bank.

There was determined opposition and heavy fighting for the rest of the day on March 24th, but the men of the Highland Division were pushing steadily on. Although Rees itself was not yet clear the advance to the North was going well, and, by midnight, a company of the 7th Battalion the Argyll and Sutherland Highlanders had reached Bienan. By that evening the fury of our attack had forced the enemy to commit his 15th Panzer Grenadier Division against the Corps.

Early that morning the Highland Division had the misfortune to lose its Divisional Commander, Major General TG Rennie, CB, DSO, MBE, who was killed by a shell splinter on the Eastern bank of the Rhine, after visiting his Brigade HQs.

Major General Rennie had commanded the 3rd Division during the invasion, and took command of the 51st Highland Division, in which he had once been a Battalion Commander, in Normandy. His high regard was expressed by one of the Highland Division men, who said, "Aye, he was a guid General. He wasna a shouting kind of man. The men liked his style and they had a lot of confidence in him".

The most spectacular event of the day had been the arrival of the huge airborne forces. Scheduled to land from ten o'clock onwards, the 18th Airborne Corps appeared dead on time. From all directions mighty streams of aircraft converged on to the area North West of Wesel. This immense air armada consisted of over four thousand aircraft, including 1,200 fighters employed on fighter sweeps. These alone claimed 93 German aeroplanes destroyed and another 16 damaged.

It was the task of the airborne troops to seize intact the bridges over the River Ijssel, after which they were to link up with the troops of the Second Army. The operation was a complete success. Three important bridges over the Ijssel were captured undamaged, and, by six o'clock in the evening, the Airborne Corps had linked up with the British troops on our right.

The next day was a day of more bitter fighting on the Corps front, with many stubborn counter-attacks by the Panzer Grenadiers. These were dispersed by our artillery fire, and, that night, Rees was finally cleared after a long house-to house battle. This meant that the enemy could now no longer have observation over our ferries and bridging operations.

The 9th Canadian Brigade, under the command of the 51st Highland Division, fought magnificently. One battalion put in an attack to clear the enemy from Bienan, where fierce opposition had been encountered. The Canadians finally cleared the village, incurring very heavy casualties in doing so. At the same time, the Highland Light Infantry of Canada put in a battalion attack on the village of Speldrop, which they cleared, and where they linked up with parties of the 1st Battalion, The Black Watch, who had been cut off there.

A company of the 2nd Battalion the Seaforth Highlanders, engaged in house clearing, were having trouble from a sniper in a nearby building. Major McKay, the Company Commander, decided to assault the building under cover of smoke. As soon as the smoke screen was laid, however, the sniper showed himself, waving a white flag. The men advanced to capture him while the Major fired another smoke bomb in case of treachery. This struck the wall without going off, and then, to the general surprise of everyone, ricochetted and hit the sniper fair and square on the forehead, killing him outright. The company commander took a great deal of convincing when he was informed that he had scored a bull's eye.

There was evidence that the Germans were about to reinforce their Northern sector through Emmerich from their Army in Holland, and anti-tank batteries devised a new slow torture form of firing. For sixty hours, from 8 o'clock on the evening of the 25th, the guns fired a round every few minutes, irregularly and monotonously, or selected points in the village East of Emmerich. It is not known what damage was done, but it is recorded that a German with a white flag swam across the Rhine and asked if the infernal artillery couldn't 'lay off' as he was becoming a bundle of nerves.

At midnight on the 25th the 43rd Division came into the battle, taking over the left flank of the bridgehead from the Highland Division.

The Royal Engineers had planned to build five bridges over the Rhine on the 30 Corps sector. These were to be known as "London", "Westminster", "Lambeth", "Blackfriars" and "Waterloo" bridges respectively. The first one to be completed was "Waterloo Bridge", a class 9 bridge. It was finished in the early hours of March 26th, and at half past eight the same morning "Lambeth Bridge", a class 15 Bailey bridge, was opened.

This bridge was built by 30 Corps Troops Royal Engineers, and the far end rested on one of the groins which jutted out into the river. By using this the bridge had been shortened by 400 feet, but even so, it was a big affair some 1,160 feet long. It was necessary to recce the groin early on to confirm that it was suitable and to check it for mines. Major P. S. Baines, the 11th Field Company Commander, took a special recce party across which included a detachment from No 4 Dog Platoon, Royal Engineers. In spite of the continuous shellfire, the dogs did useful work in seeking out the few mines that were there.

The Sappers had done their work well under the trying conditions of being under fire in an exposed position, and everything had gone according to plan.

When the bridge was completed the sappers were almost too tired to stand, but, together with their old team-mates, the 44th Company of the Pioneer Corps, who had been their partners since Normandy, they cheerfully crossed the bridge to tackle fresh engineering tasks on the other side of the Rhine.

On the same day the Prime Minister and his party, which included Field Marshal Sir Bernard Montgomery and Field Marshal Sir Alan Brook, the Chief of the Imperial General Staff, crossed the Rhine in Buffaloes. Mr Churchill congratulated the men in a short speech, at the close of which Field Marshal Montgomery suggested to the troops: "Go on, ask him for a cigar".

At this time, amongst the wreckage of buildings near the river, Rear 30 Corps noticed a large bronze boar — an animal identical with the 30 Corps flash, save that it was resting and not rampant. Thinking that it would be an excellently symbolic memorial to be set up in the Corps final resting place in Germany, it was liberated and placed in its own light trailer under the personal care of a sergeant specially detailed for the task. The boar had suffered from the attention of Typhoons: its lower jaw and one tusk were missing and it had many small holes in its body, but one of the Corps workshops carried out a skilful job of plastic surgery and the "Pig" was a prominent and popular sight in the subsequent advance of "Rear".

The 43rd Division now entered into its first battle East of the Rhine, when men of the Division attacked the town of Millingen lying about five miles North of Rees. After difficult fighting the town was won, and scattered farm buildings in the area cleared.

That night, the 51st Highland Division attacked towards Ijsselberg, and captured intact the important bridge on the main exit from Rees. The village of Empel was taken, three SP guns being knocked out and one severely damaged, all by Piats. The way was now clear for the attack on Ijsselberg.

Meanwhile work had gone ahead on the Class 40 bridges, and at midnight that night, the 26th/27th March, the first of them, "London Bridge", was completed.

The Corps Commander now planned to get each Division on a narrow front so that the enemy could be attacked incessantly

MEN OF THE 3RD BRITISH DIVISION MOPPING UP GERMAN SNIPERS IN LINGEN

day and night. On March 27th the 3rd British Division crossed the river and took over part of the right hand sector of the bridgehead from the 51st Highland Division, while the 3rd Canadian Division took over part of the left hand sector from the 43rd Division. Now began a period of incessant hammering of the enemy's defences, with the object of preparing the way for an armoured break-out Northeast into Germany.

On the morning of the 27th the 4th and 5th Battalions of the Wiltshire Regiment (43rd Division) advanced against fairly light opposition until the area of the unfinished autobahn was reached. Here, however, they discovered a strong defence line, an intricate trench system with some concrete fieldworks, which was strongly held by the enemy who was well armed with many automatic weapons. That afternoon the 1st Battalion, the Worcestershire Regiment, and the 7th Battalion, the Somerset Light Infantry, attacked but were held up for several hours by the vicious machine-gun fire. Finally, after a heavy exchange of fire, the defence line was over-run, and the line of the autobahn was reached and held.

The weather, which had been unusually fine for the start of the operation, had changed, and the familiar rain was back again, turning the minor roads into mud tracks. At one time a road near Millingen which was being used as a main axis by both the Canadians and the 43rd Division, was in danger of collapsing completely under the strain. Voluntary road repairing parties gathered from nearby units and set to work filling in the deep muddy ruts. Majors and troopers took off their jackets and set to work with a will to keep the road open so that the advance could go on without delay. They collected bricks and rubble from shattered buildings and by continuous work managed to keep the road in fairly reasonable condition.

In spite of the bad going progress went on and on March 28th advances were made all along the perimeter of the bridgehead. The 3rd British Division took Haldern, the Highland Division entered Ijsselberg, while the 43rd Division captured Megehelen. The 3rd Canadian Division, which had taken Dornick and Vrasselt, passed to the command of the 2nd Canadian Corps at midday.

The attack on Ijsselberg was supported by a squadron of tanks of the Sherwood Rangers Yeomanry. It was found that the enemy had blown both bridges over the river and had erected massive road blocks protected by mines in the streets. The Engineers set to work to clear the mines and to bridge the river. They worked under severe shellfire as the enemy had the approaches to the bridges well registered.

The tanks were exposed all day to the concentrated shellfire ot the enemy, but casualties were light among the personnel. Several tanks were hit and in the light of one of the burning vehicles a small figure was seen crouching in a shell hole, cooking a teutonic chicken. This turned out to be Trooper McCavish preparing a meal for the tank commander, Lieutenant Hyde, and probably explained how Mr Hyde was able to keep his comfortable figure under all the stresses of battle.

At dawn on the 29th the Squadron was able to cross the river over a Bailey bridge which the Engineers had completed during the night, and joined up again with the infantry.

Further up the road from Ijsselberg some infantry had established their headquarters in a farmstead, and had ordered the unwilling inhabitants to go back to Ijsselberg. That evening they were surprised to see the whole female contingent returning in single file, each carrying a large pail. Shells were falling in the vicinity, but the women happily and unconcernedly sat down to their daily tasks of milking the cows. This done, the women returned, again in single file, leaving behind them a herd of contented cows and a collection of slightly shaken infantrymen.

Megehelen had been taken only after great difficulty. Stiff fire from German 88 millimetres forced the infantry to abandon their armoured troop carriers and advance on foot. Flamethrowers, supporting men of the 5th Battalion the Duke of Cornwall's Light Infantry, were bogged on the way in, and only one got through to fire the houses and burn out the enemy.

The autobahn defence line and the village of Megehelen proved to be the main cores of resistance on the left flank of the bridgehead. Fighting had been furious, and there had been several occasions when the fanatical Nazis shot their comrades who were attempting to surrender.

Further up the Rhine and its tributaries there had been big advances. A Second Army column had pushed through Haltern and reached Dulmen; the Ninth U. S. Army had captured Duisburg; and the First U. S. Army had pushed on to Marburg. On the left the Second Canadian Corps was preparing for an attack on Emmerich, and by midnight were within a mile of the town. It appeared certain that the German collapse in the West had begun.

On March 29th, 30 Corps pushed steadily ahead, and the 43rd Division captured the important road centre of Anholt. They secured crossings over the streams North of the town, while the Royal Engineers bridged the numerous streams and road craters. Further to the East the 3rd British Division, supported by two squadrons of the 22nd Dragoons and one squadron of the 141st Regiment R. A. C., captured Werth.

The 51st Highland Division, having taken Ijsselberg, now pushed on and secured a crossing of the River Aa, just South of Dinxperloo. They later cleared the town of Dinxperloo, and thus secured the vital axis for the subsequent armoured advance which was to take place the next day.

Meanwhile the Royal Engineers concluded their programme of bridging the Rhine. "Blackfriars Bridge" had been opened at noon on the 28th, and on the evening of the 29th, the last of them, "Westminster Bridge", was ready, having been completed, without the slightest hitch, in 32 hours. General Sir Miles Dempsey, Commander of the Second Army, officially opened "Westminster Bridge" and told the Sappers that the Rhine battle was won, and that the bridges they had built would allow the armour to get across and tear the heart out of Germany. During the task the Royal Engineers had 155 all ranks killed and wounded.

30 Corps was now poised and ready for the final round, and the enemy's resistance, although stubborn, had been broken. By the evening of the 29th of March we had taken 2,750 prisoners, and had inflicted heavy casualties. The enemy's last good remaining defence line on the River Ijssel had been secured, and, further North, a crossing had been made over the River Aa. There were now no major natural obstacles for a considerable distance, and the old pig was ready to take advantage of the situation and push Club Route a long way towards its goal.

THE FINAL ROUND.

APPROX. LINE AT 13 APRIL 45.

SCALE 1 : 1,400,000.

0 10 20 30
Miles

CHAPTER ELEVEN

THE FINAL ROUND

On Good Friday, March 30th, the troops of 30 Corps were waiting for the signal to begin the break-out from the bridge-head. The tanks of the Guards Armoured Division were now across the Rhine, and the stage was set for the last battles.

The enemy had thrown in his strongest forces to oppose our advance, and, as a result, our progress had been slower than that of our right flanking Corps. Already, the armour of the Second Army was surging forward to the outskirts of Munster against negligible resistance. But now it was 30 Corps' turn to make a big stride ahead. We were to break out of our bridgehead and advance as mobile protection for the left flank of the Second Army.

Accordingly, the Guards Armoured Division was directed to push forward on the axis Groenlo — Enschede — Quakenbruck — Bremen. As left flank protection during this advance, an armoured column of the 43rd Division, and its old partner the 8th Armoured Brigade, was to break out of the Anholt area, while the 3rd British Division was to follow the tanks of the Guards as immediate Corps reserve. The Highland Division, meanwhile, was to have a well-deserved rest in the Ijsselburg area. As the Guards passed through the 51st Highland Division's positions, the men stood up and cheered, the Jocks calling out, "Mind the paint!"

On our left flank, Emmerich had fallen to the Canadians, and the Canadian Army was now ready to push onwards to the Zuyder Zee and clear Northern Holland.

Early on this Good Friday morning the Armoured Division started its drive, led by the Grenadier Guards Group. It soon became evident that the two German divisions opposing our advance, the 6th and 8th Parachute Divisions, known as "The Ugly Sisters", were conducting a hurried withdrawal action. The roads were badly cratered, and every small town was held. The Grenadiers had some stiff fighting to take Aalten, where they found all the main bridges blown, but a small bridge to the East of the town was discovered intact, and, by nightfall, the armour was well on the way to Lichtenvoorde.

In an effort to patch up his battered divisions, the enemy was taking extreme measures. A German broadcast heard on March 30th stated that the Fuhrer had ordered the establishment of a volunteer Corps, and had agreed to allow it to bear his name. "At the hour of extreme danger which threatens the homeland", it was said, "the Volunteer Corps, Adolph Hitler, will be formed to attack and destroy the enemy spearheads, to carry out demolitions, and to destroy the enemy wherever he might be met".

In these last days of the Reich, the Germans made an effort to emulate the Resistance Movements of the Occupied Countries, and the "Werewolf" movement was also formed. The title was taken from a novel of that name which described the guerilla activities by German peasants in the 30 Years War, and the sign of the movement was a 'Wolfsangel'. It was expected that the romantic associations with the name 'Werewolf' would appeal to German youth, while the 'Wolfsangel' sign, chalked on walls and Allied vehicles, would be a successful counter to our 'V' sign. Although the movement was heralded so hopefully, it did, in fact, come to nothing at all.

The scene in Anholt as dawn broke that day was one of tremendous activity. The little town was filled with Sherman tanks of the 8th Armoured Brigade and the men of the Wessex Regiments who were to ride on them, while Kangaroos, anti-tank guns, armoured cars, Bren carriers, trucks and Jeeps filled all the available parking places.

By degrees, the traffic in Anholt straightened itself out, and, as the morning passed, the long lines of vehicles strung out to the northeast, towards the first objectives, which were the canal bridges at Varsseveld and Ruurlo.

Our advance was being made roughly parallel to the German—Dutch border, and, soon after leaving Anholt, the troops found themselves once again in Holland. This proved confusing to the troops, who wished to respect the property of the Dutch, but had little regard for anything German.

Pockets of enemy parachutists were soon being overrun, and at times the scene resembled a fox-hunt, with innumerable foxes, as the tanks chased in all directions after the fleeing Huns.

An armoured runabout of the Sherwood Rangers Yeomanry thrust inadvertantly into enemy territory with Captain G. S. T. Leinster and Sergeant-Major Taylor aboard. The road was straight, and a speed of 50 miles an hour was being maintained, when they suddenly ran into a party of Germans. The surprise was mutual, but fortunately Corporal Rodde, the driver, thought faster than the Huns, and backed his car out of danger at high speed before the Germans had recovered from their surprise.

By that evening Sinderen had been cleared, and the tanks were making for Varsseveld. The RAF had had a good day shooting up enemy movement on the roads ahead, and had wrought tremendous havoc.

Soon after nine o'clock the next morning the Grenadier Guards Group entered Lichtenvoorde, and in the early afternoon reached Groenlo, which they reported clear. They pursued the retiring 8th Parachute Division up the road towards Eibergen, but did not succeed in catching up with the main body. The bridge North of Eibergen was captured intact, and at dusk the Grenadiers were clearing the town, while further North the Irish Guards were fighting in Neede.

Varsseveld was cleared of the enemy in the early morning, but in many cases small pockets of the enemy had been left close to the newly-opened route. A troop of the 43rd Reconnaissance Regiment, probing out to a flank near Sinderen, came under fire from a multi-barrelled 20mm anti-tank gun, supported by Spandaus. The leading armoured car, commanded by Sergeant Hall, was peppered with 20mm shot, but was not put out of action. Sergeant Hall continued to engage at close range, and his gunner used his machine-gun to such good effect that the anti-tank gun was knocked out and the entire crew incapacitated. For his part in this action, Sergeant Hall was awarded the Military Medal.

The following day, Easter Sunday, while the good people of Holland were going to church, the stream of armoured cars and tanks flowed on towards Hengelo. The routes of the Guards Armoured Division and the 43rd Division column crossed at times when diversions had to be made to avoid blown bridges. Traffic blocks frequently occurred, but these were quickly straightened out, and the advance went on.

Earlier that morning, a squadron of the 4th/7th Dragoon Guards had got through Halle without opposition and was nearing Ruurlo before dawn came. Approaching a bridge South of the town, they saw a light ahead of them. The leading troop commander, Lieutenant Peter Kirk, and Sergeant Haymer of the 4th Somersets, went forward on foot to investigate. It was lucky they did so, for on the bridge were two 500 pound bombs and twenty-four Teller mines, all wired up ready for firing. The Sergeant went forward and unfixed the contraption, well aware that the enemy might explode it at any moment. A thousand yards further on, another bunch of mines was found, and again the intrepid Sergeant Haymer dealt with the situation. At the end of the day, the 43rd Division column had reached the Twente Canal at Lochem and Diepenheim,

Meanwhile, the Coldstream Guards Group had led the Armoured Division by subsidiary roads, hoping to reach the bridge over the Twente Canal between Enschede and Hengelo and capture it intact. The leading troop of tanks actually reached the bridge and crossed it, but, as soon as they were over, the bridge was blown. Three of the four tanks that had crossed were knocked out, but most of the crews escaped by swimming back over the canal. The fourth tank went on alone, worked its way back to Enschede, and joined up with the remainder of the Coldstream Group, who had, meanwhile, reached Enschede.

From Enschede, the Guards were able to push forward to a point northeast of Hengelo, where a unit of the Coldstream Group spent a pleasant evening picking off German staff cars, which were making a hurried exit from the outflanked town.

Unable to secure a quick crossing of the Twente Canal, the 43rd Division sent the 130th Brigade round the end of the canal at Enschede. After a long, forced march by night in heavy rain, during which tanks and other tracked vehicles had to tow the wheeled vehicles through the mud, the Brigade passed through Enschede and mounted the attack on Hengelo.

Attacking from the Southeast along the main road, supported by tanks of the Sherwood Rangers, the 5th Dorsets met only light opposition. They pressed on into the town, and tank crews soon reported that they were held up, not by the enemy, but by the cheering crowds of Dutch people, who were giving them a tremendous welcome.

The capture of Hengelo cut the railway from Hannover to Amsterdam, which was being used as a "V-2" supply route. The celebrations of the liberated people increased in intensity during the day, and whole platoons were disappearing, willingly or unwillingly, to take part in the rejoicing. Crowds of small children were searching wistfully for a "Tommee" to take home and entertain, but, unfortunately, there were not enough soldiers to go round.

Meanwhile, on the evening of April 2nd, tanks of the Guards Armoured Division, crossing the border into Germany, captured Nordhorn. They managed to cross the River Vecht by a weak bridge, which took most of the tanks before collapsing, and, just before midnight, the Scots Guards climbed onto the Cromwell tanks, and set off down the road leading to the bridge across the River Ems at Lingen.

This dramatic midnight dash took them right through the German lines, and many German positions were shot up as they raced by. They stopped short of the bridge, and two platoons, approaching it silently, got safely across, but, as the first tanks moved up, the bridge was blown.

The 2nd Household Cavalry Regiment, who, during the last two days, had been shooting up the withdrawing columns of the enemy, reported a bridge just North of Lingen to be intact, but in enemy hands. Accordingly, a company of the 5th Coldstream Guards was ordered to capture the bridge, if possible, before it was destroyed.

On his preliminary reconnaissance, the Company Commander, Captain Ian Liddell, discovered that the bridge was prepared for demolition, with four 500 pound bombs lying on it, two at either end. The bridge was covered by a force of about 150 enemy infantry, supported by at least two SP guns and two 20 mm anti-tank guns.

Captain Liddell realised that if the enemy spotted troops running across the bridge, they would at once blow it up. He therefore decided that he must risk crossing the bridge alone to cut the wires connecting the bombs to the detonators.

He ordered the company to advance on either side of an embanked road which led up to the bridge, but before the first platoon had reached a point from which they could give him covering fire, Captain Liddell dashed boldly forward, armed with a pair of wire cutters.

He climbed a ten foot high barricade which was blocking the entry to the bridge, then, under extremely heavy fire, he dashed across the bridge, a distance of at least a hundred yards, and cut the wires attached to the far pair of bombs. He then sped back, and cut the wires of the bombs on the near side.

He was about to lead his men in an attack, when he was told that four more bombs had been located underneath the bridge. Without hesitation, he ran back again and cut the wires attached to these. Then he climbed onto the barricade, and, standing there in full view of the enemy, signalled his company to advance.

Inspired by his example, the men charged across, accounted for the enemy, and the bridge was seized intact. The capture of the bridge was entirely due to the magnificent bravery of Captain Liddell. He was, at times, a sitting target at a range of not more than twenty yards, and that he escaped injury is little short of a miracle. He was awarded the Victoria Cross, but, unfortunately, in a later action, he was killed.

The Coldstream Group, having crossed the Ems by this bridge, pushed on Southwards and cleared the area between the River Ems and the Dortmund-Ems Canal.

Meanwhile, the 185th Infantry Brigade of the 3rd British Division, had been reconnoitring the Canal and River at a point South of Lingen, prior to making an assault crossing there. When it became known that the Coldstream Guards had captured the Northern bridge intact, the Brigade Commander changed his plan, and decided to make his crossing there. The Brigade crossed the Coldstream bridge, and then, in the darkness, launched an assault on the Dortmund-Ems Canal, which was stubbornly defended by the enemy.

After some very bitter fighting, they managed to get across and successfully completed their mission. This assault crossing, carried out as it was in the dark, was a fine achievement on the part of the 185th Brigade.

There then followed 48 hours of stiff fighting for Lingen, with the 3rd Division opposed by two battle groups, the 7th Parachute Division and the Grossdeutschland Training Brigade, but finally the enemy was accounted for and the town taken.

The 9th Brigade of the 3rd Division then moved Southwards on the far bank of the Canal, opened another crossing about 5 miles from Lingen, and established contact with the 51st Highland Division, which had come forward on the right flank from Enschede.

In Lingen, good use was made of the telephone exchange, which was found in working order. On one occasion, it was found possible to get in touch with the German Army HQ. Taking the role of the German Commander of Lingen, we reported that the British had been thrown back across the river. German Army HQ were delighted with this good news, and, in their turn, they told us that they were on the move.

With a view to giving the RAF a glorious target, we enquired their destination, but, at this, they became cautious. "Send a special DR, and we will tell you", they said, after a long pause. This offer, regretfully, had to be declined. It was unfortunate that the Germans had been so well trained in line security.

On our left flank, the advance was going well, and the Canadians had reached Meppen. Startling progress had been made by the armoured divisions of the Second Army on our right flank. Having crossed the Ems-Weser Canal on a broad front, they had now reached the little town of Liebenau, on the River Weser, a point only 25 miles from Hannover.

A pause now became necessary while we built bridges at Lingen, and this gave the enemy a chance to collect himself a little. The traffic difficulties in the battered town were considerable, for the congestion in the restricted streets, as the Divisions flooded forward, caused many traffic blocks.

INFANTRY OF THE 52ND LOWLAND DIVISION MOPPING UP THE DOCK AREA OF BREMEN

The Corps advanced from the town on two routes, but rapid progress was prevented by the resistance of the German paratroopers. A proper attack had to be mounted against every village, and the demolitions, road blocks and mines, covered in every case by determined rearguards, held us up considerably.

However, by April 10th, the Guards had reached Bippen and Menslage, while on the Northern route, the 43rd Division had secured crossings over the River Hase, and captured the town of Haselunne. On the same day, the 3rd British Division passed to the command of 12 Corps, and moved away from our sector.

The Corps advance was well supported by the RAF during this period, for the weather was good, and the fighter bombers made full use of every opportunity to strike at the retiring enemy.

We were now over-running hordes of non-German slave labour. Frenchmen and Belgians predominated, although there were large numbers of Russians and Poles. It was expected that German espionage Gestapo agents would probably be mixed up among them, and our Security Police had their hands full checking their identity.

On April 11th, the Corps Commander decided to continue the advance on a three Divisional front, with the 51st Highland Division on the right, the Guards in the centre, and the 43rd Division on the left.

Moving North from Lohne to Vechta, the leading car troop of the Derbyshire Yeomanry, the 51st Reconnaissance Regiment, found a large crater in the road three miles South of the town. It was a very large crater, and one which would have taken several hours to fill or bridge. However, the carrier sections managed to get round it, and a party consisting of an officer and 15 men decided to push on and attempt to rush the main objective, the bridge in the centre of Vechta.

On nearing the bridge, they came under heavy Spandau fire, but, although the odds were heavy against our men, they pushed on, and the bridge was crossed. Boche paratroopers now appeared, and further progress became impossible. The situation was becoming very uncomfortable when the reassuring rumble of approaching tanks was heard, and a squadron of Shermans came into sight. They were followed by men of the 7th Battalion of the Argyll and Sutherland Highlanders. The opposition was now quickly overcome, and, by nightfall, the town was in our hands.

The 43rd Division was entrusted with the task of capturing the important road and rail centre of Cloppenburg. With this town captured, the final cutting of German communications between Holland and Bremen would be achieved.

In the early afternoon of April 13th, the 7th Battalion, the Hampshire Regiment, began the assault, supported by tanks of the Sherwood Rangers Yeomanry. Advancing along two routes, they reached the demolished river bridge in the centre of the town, and another bridge to the North of it, before the enemy reacted.

Stiff fighting was soon taking place against a strong force of young Nazis, amongst whom were elements of the Grossdeutschland Brigade, Hitler's so-called bodyguard. Fighting went on until dark, and the enemy had to be driven out house by house. As they pulled out, the Germans were further engaged by the 5th Battalion, the Duke of Cornwall's Light Infantry, who had made a flanking movement to the North of the town. A complete German company, a hundred strong, surrendered to them.

The fighting had been very bitter, with the enemy ready to take advantage of any target which presented itself. In the heat of battle an indignant message was passed over the wireless to the world in general by Corporal McDonald, from his tank. Said he:

"Every time I put my loaf out for a shufti, some blinker draws a bead on me".

The next day, the 1st Battalion, the Worcestershire Regiment, faced the first counter-attack since the break-out from the Rhine bridgehead. With the crossroads at Ahlhorn as its objective, this Battalion, with strong armoured support, advanced along a badly cratered road in a persistent downpour of rain. A small river bridge was found to be blown, but two platoons got across to engage the enemy on the far bank. Meanwhile, an alternative crossing was found, and the whole Battalion got over and provided cover for the subsequent bridging operation by the Royal Engineers.

The Germans then reacted strongly. The bridging was stopped by heavy and accurate shellfire, and then the area in which the Worcestershires had consolidated was subjected to intense shelling. The enemy counter-attack followed immediately afterwards, and our two forward platoons were overrun. But our men rallied well, the counter-attack was halted, and then smashed. After an hour's fierce fighting, the Germans pulled back, leaving behind them many prisoners and dead.

Corps Headquarters suffered a great loss on April 14th, when the Brigadier 'Q', Brigadier G. Webb CBE DSO, was killed in a motor accident while returning from a conference. He was driving his own car, and a bump in the road, near Lingen, caused him to swerve into a tree.

Meanwhile, the Guards Armoured Division had reached Emstek, and the Highlanders had stormed into Quakenbruck and Hanstedt. The Guards were now withdrawn, and came under the command of 12 Corps. They had been engaged in some sort of fighting every day since crossing the Rhine.

During our advance, lorry drivers of the RASC were working full out, keeping the Divisions supplied with ammunition, food, bridging materials, mail and stores. Some drivers were averaging 250 miles a day, but they kept going cheerfully, in spite of the strain of driving over the dreadful roads and getting insufficient sleep. The spirit was: "Let's give those blokes in front what they want to do the job, and get the damn war over quickly".

The main thrust of the Second Army was now directed North Eastwards, with 8 Corps advancing on Lubeck, and 12 Corps on Hamburg. The role of 30 Corps was still to protect the left flank of the Second Army, and to advance on Bremen from the South and South West. The 3rd British Division came under the command of 30 Corps again, and was given the task of capturing Brinkum and Delmenhorst. The Corps' bag of prisoners since crossing the Rhine was over 10,000, and now the stage was set for the knock-out blow.

Further South, the whole system of water defences in the West had collapsed. The Rhine, the Ems, the Weser and the Aller had all been breached, and now the Americans were across the Elbe, the last great barrier before Berlin. At four points they were only 100 miles from the Russian front, while Berlin itself was only 50 miles from the foremost columns of the US Army.

It was obvious that German higher strategy had now neither meaning nor future, and the end could not be long delayed. From the East, the Russian Armies were rapidly approaching Berlin. The West Wall had collapsed, and it was clear that the East Wall would soon give way as well.

At this stage, no doubt, Hitler recollected, with misgiving, his sweeping statement in Mein Kampf:

"When, due to acts of a few scoundrels, the body of a nation visibly disintegrates, refusal to obey those men may make it possible to save a nation from ruin, while continued obedience would be mania".

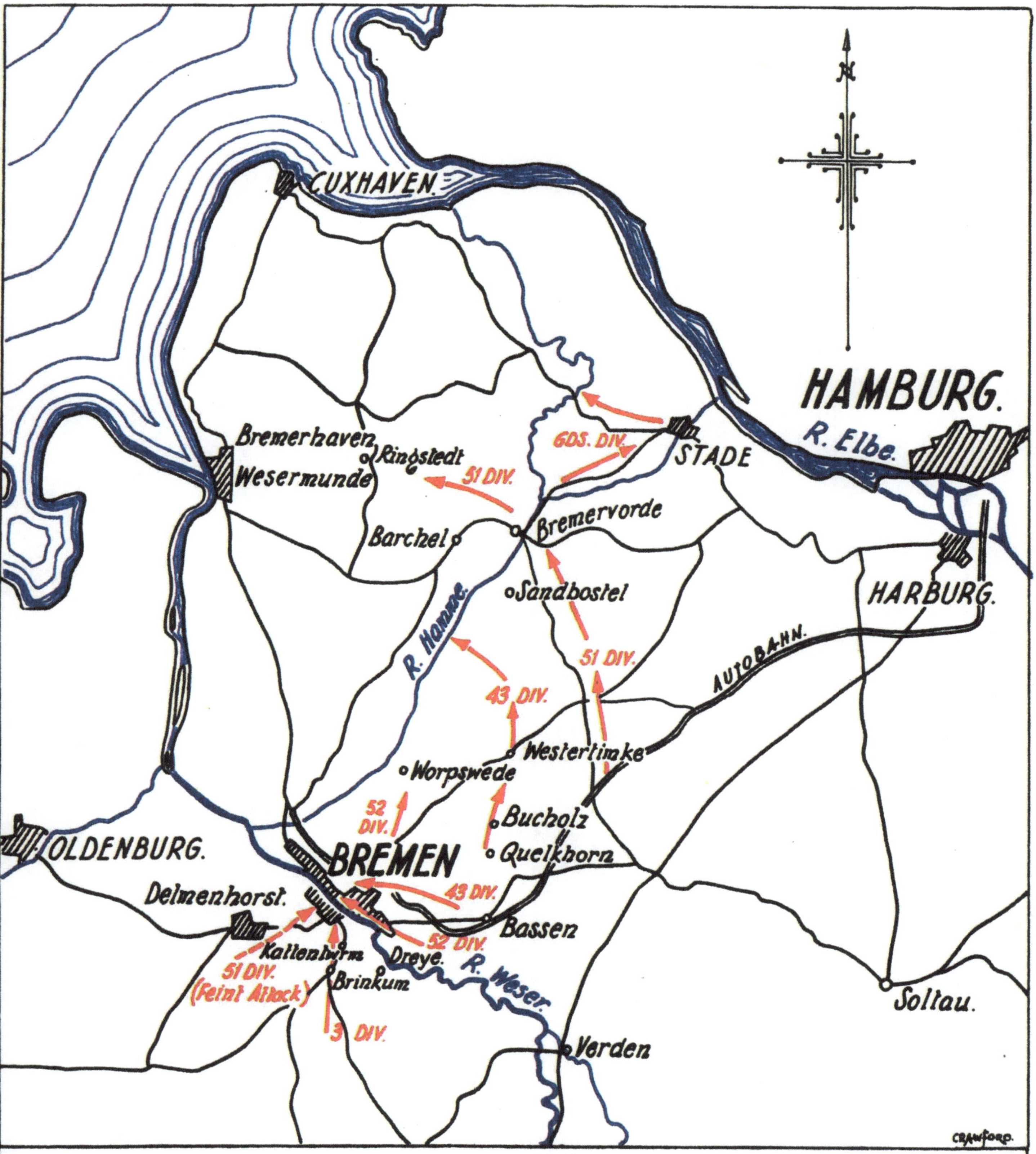

THE KNOCK-OUT.

SCALE 1: 700,000.

0 10 20

· Miles ·

CHAPTER TWELVE

THE KNOCK OUT

The once lovely city of Bremen, with its pre-war population of half a million, lies on both sides of the River Weser. Next to Hamburg it is the largest port in Germany, and before the war the docks handled an export trade of three million tons a year. It is a city steeped in history, and with its sister ports of Hamburg and Lubeck, once formed part of the Hanseatic League, which was created in the Middle Ages by merchants in North West Germany for the purpose of mutual defence against piracy in the North Sea and the Baltic, and for the furtherance of mutual trade interests.

There is a clear cut division between the Altstadt, the old town, and the remainder of the city. The Altstadt lies on the North bank of the Weser, while the Neustadt, the new town, is on the South bank, but expansion has been mainly on the North side. There are, in addition to the U boat pens, which had received so much attention from the RAF, the huge Focke Wulf aircraft factory, the Atlas works, and many other large factories.

Shipping and ship-building were the most important industries, the Nord Deutscher Lloyd Line operated from this port, and owned the two famous transatlantic liners Bremen and Europa.

To the North East of Bremen, and between the estuaries of the rivers Weser and Elbe lies the rural country of the Cuxhaven Peninsular. On the Eastern bank of the Weser, where the river widens to meet the sea, is the port of Bremerhaven, the out-port for Bremen, and at the Northern tip of the peninsula is the Naval base, fishing port, and holiday resort of Cuxhaven.

It was to Bremen in mid-April that the hard fighting remnants of the German Parachute Regiments withdrew before 30 Corps' advance, and it was to Bremen that Club Route was destined to lead.

The 3rd British Division, approaching from the South, became engaged on April 15th in bitter fighting in the town of Brinkum. Here an SS Training Battalion, consisting of hot-headed youths whose ages ranged from 14 to 18, put up a fanatical resistance. They were led by competent NCOs, and fighting alongside them were U boat crews from Bremen. In the house-to-house fighting this motley collection fought against the Norfolks and the Warwicks like seasoned warriors, and it was not until April 17th that the town was finally cleared, and then only after it had been practically burnt to the ground by flame-throwers.

As the 3rd British Division was fully committed in the fighting for Brinkum, the Corps Commander decided to push the 51st Highland Division towards Delmenhorst. A Brigade attack was planned, but on the morning of April 20th there was reason to believe that the enemy would not defend the town. Accordingly a squadron of the Derbyshire Yeomanry, 51st Reconnaissance Regiment, was ordered to probe into the town.

Approaching the outskirts they captured a few prisoners, and the only other incident was when one of the armoured cars struck a mine. It seemed unbelievable that a town of this size was going to be yielded without a fight, but within half an hour the squadron had entered the town and secured the several bridges without meeting any opposition at all. The reason for the surrender became clear when it was found that a large number of German wounded were in the fifteen hospitals there. The Recce squadron, which had expected a fight, received instead quite a welcome from the inhabitants.

Further South a squadron of the 3rd Reconnaissance Regiment was advancing along a thickly mined road. The road was under fire, but Sergeant Falkener of the 17th Field Company, Royal Engineers, who was attached to the squadron, distinguished himself by going forward and removing a number of mines. Later he screened and protected wounded men from the enemy small arms fire by driving his half-track across the road in front of them. His extremely gallant conduct assisted the squadron to reach their objective, and won for him the Military Medal.

In a little town near Bremen on April 20th tank crews were startled to see a German Admiral, in full regalia, gravely going round the tanks, and asking after the crews' welfare. It was noticed that he had a strong London accent, and the "Admiral" turned out to be Sergeant Roberts of the Sherwood Rangers Yeomanry, accompanied by Trooper Turner, acting as his ADC. Local inhabitants, who were mostly retired mariners from Bremen and Bremerhaven, watched the pantomime in complete bewilderment.

On the same day a Field Regiment fired 400 rounds into Bremen containing leaflets with the following text:

"The choice is yours. The British Army is lying outside Bremen, supported by the RAF, and is about to capture the city. There are two ways in which this can take place. Either by the employment of all the means at the disposal of the Army and the RAF, or by the occupation of the town after unconditional surrender. The choice is yours as to which course is followed. Yours is the responsibility for the unnecessary bloodshed which will result if you choose the first way. Otherwise you must send an envoy under the protection of a white flag over to the British lines. You have 24 hours in which to decide".

Meanwhile the 52nd Lowland Division, which had crossed the Weser with 12 Corps, came under our command again, and began to close in on Bremen from the South East.

When they reached Achim it was found that the telephone exchange was working, and the opportunity was taken to carry the war of nerves on Bremen a stage further. A message was passed to the Army Commander in the City, and he was told that at that very moment the all-out assault was beginning. Synchronised to the very second, the first wave of bombers passed overhead to attack the city. The German Commander was told that, if at any time he wished to surrender there would be someone on the telephone to discuss the matter with him.

The success of the war of nerves was confirmed when General Becker later told how he had been invited to a party during the last days of the battle by some of the leading industrialists of the city. They gave him a royal time, and then one of them said to the General: "I suppose you will soon be looking for a new job"?

When he agreed, they said they could probably find him a good post in one of their firms. But they pointed out that if the battle went on much longer, the Bremen industrial area would be wiped out, and in that case there would be not the slightest chance of providing him with a post. But, if Bremen surrendered, they suggested . . . . . .

At this point the General realised what they were getting at. "Heil Hitler", he shouted furiously, and left the room in high dudgeon.

The 43rd Wessex Division now crossed the Weser and moved to the Verden area to prepare for an assault on the city from the East. The divisions closed relentlessly on the city, and on April 23rd, as they had not surrendered, the investment began. The 130 Brigade cleared the difficult wooded country between Ahausen and Dauelsen, and on the following day the 43rd Division reached and cut the Bremen—Hamburg Autobahn near Bassen.

During this operation the Wessex Division were unlucky to run up against a Nebelwerfer training school, who gave a good example of their training.

About this time an armoured recce unit had the pleasure of capturing Belli's Monster Circus. Three lions had been brewed up, and two bears escaped into the woods, but a couple of elephants were captured intact, and several clowns taken prisoner. This circus is now providing entertainment for our own troops.

On our right flank the armour had reached the area of Harburg, and cut the last road into Hamburg South of the Elbe. The 7th Armoured Division received an ambassador in the shape of a wizened little Teuton, who cycled furiously into their lines, and produced a letter addressed to the "British Armeecommander — not for the hands of Nazis". This letter stated that certain citizens of Hamburg had had enough war, and proposed to hold a great peace jamboree, and would the British kindly refrain from bombing the town while the peace picnic was being held. As it was thought that it was probably a ruse to safeguard the erection of a V—5, the request was not complied with.

The Canadians on our left had a bridgehead over the Kustern Canal West of Oldenburg, and were firmly established. The Russian Army had been very successful in its attack, and was now both North and South of Berlin.

The attack on the South Western defences of Bremen went exactly according to plan. It was arranged for the 51st Highland Division to carry out a feint attack from the Delmenhorst area where the ground was not flooded, and where the enemy would naturally expect an attack. The main effort was to be made by the 3rd British Division which was to put in a surprise attack over the floods in Buffaloes. The enemy would hardly expect us to attack across water when a good approach was available over dry land. Having penetrated into the town the 3rd Division was to turn outwards, and take the main German defences opposite Delmenhorst in the rear.

The 3rd British Division attacked on the night of the 24th/25th. The ground was flooded to a depth of about three feet, and the 4th Royal Tank Regiment provided the necessary Buffaloes to carry the men of the 2nd Royal Ulster Rifles and the 2nd Royal Warwicks. They made a total of 115 trips before ferrying ceased. Flamethrowers of the 7th Royal Tank Regiment supported the infantry, and gave great assistance.

A troop of the 4th/7th Dragoon Guards, commanded by Lieutenant D Wicks was supporting the infantry, and tried to get into the village of Dreye. A road block, and a bunch of Germans in a large factory building close by, barred their progress. After a vain attempt had been made to destroy the block by gunfire, a Petard tank was brought up, and hurled its huge missile at the block, which was blown to bits. Crocodile tanks then passed through, waddling along the road, with their trailers bobbing along behind. Then sheet after sheet of yellow flame poured into the factory, lighting the scene so that even the moon grew pale. After a minute of this the Crocodile troop commander reported on his wireless: "That's fixed them, they're coming out now, dozens of them". They were: about 50 bedraggled Huns ran out on the road with their hands up. This ended resistance in the village.

The infantry reached Kattenturm, and then advanced across the ruins of the Focke Wulf factory to penetrate deep into the Southern outskirts of Bremen, capturing another 1,000 prisoners.

The complete success of the plan was now apparent, for the enemy were taken by surprise, and the main German defences on that side were overrun. As one captured German officer said to Lieutenant Ken Bradshaw, the IO of the 2nd Royal Ulster Rifles. "It was Military Science par excellence." General Becker, German Commander of the Bremen defences, thought it was not quite playing the game. When he was captured a little later, he confirmed the success of our plan by saying that the main attack came in on the right. This was, of course, the feint attack. He said: "Then you put your soldiers into the Verdammte Schwimmpanzer, and you came up behind us. It was unfair".

This was the last battle the 3rd Division was to fight on the Continent. An assault division on the Normandy beaches, they had fought a series of brillant battles, culminating in this particularly successful operation. Later, they received the following message from the Corps Commander, Lt Gen. BG Horrocks CB DSO MC:

> "As I started the war commanding a Battalion in the 3rd Division, nothing can give me greater pleasure than to see it in such fine fettle at the end. Well done, 3rd Division"!

The 52nd Division was penetrating deeply into the South Eastern portion of the town, and had broken through the fixed defences of Bremen on that side. After many hours of fierce street fighting, the men of the Lowland Division found the opposition weakening on the 26th, and the battle of Bremen was in its closing stages. Men of this Mountain Division, which had fought almost exclusively below sea-level on the Continent, had played a big part in the capture of the city.

A sensational surrender occured when Police General Schroder came out of his HQ and gave himself up with a thousand Bremen police.

It was the task of 129 Brigade of the 43rd Division to clear the fashionable residential area adjoining the big Burger Park, the

"Hyde Park Corner" of Bremen. In this area were the Nazi Party Headquarters, the Volksturm Headquarters, and the residences of a number of well-known personalities. It was known that the Chiefs of the Bremen forces would withdraw into this area to make their so-called last stand. Their fortresses were the massive concrete and brick surface air raid shelters, of which there were a number in the park.

On the evening of the 26th the 4th Battalion, the Somerset Light Infantry led the assault, and encountered tough opposition in the street battles that followed. Meanwhile the 4th and 5th Battalions of the Wiltshire Regiment began to clear the Burger Park itself, working their way with tanks through the park roads against only spasmodic small arms fire.

In one of the shelters Major BGP Pope, commanding a company of the 4th Wiltshires, found Major General Siber, the Bremen Garrison Commander, and his staff, and accepted his surrender. Early the next day a Wiltshire platoon had just begun to assault a small barrack area, when a party of Germans came out of what proved to be the Gun Operations Room of the Bremen Ack Ack defences, a reinforced building standing in the middle of the barracks. Entering this building, Major Pope found Lieutenant General Fritz Becker, Commander of the Bremen Defences, and a considerable number of staff officers, all of whom were disarmed and taken prisoner.

The first big German port on the North Sea to fall to the Allies had been captured with less difficulty than had been expected. With its garrison of at least 10,000 men, and its unusually fine defensive possibilities, it could have caused us a lot of trouble, but the truth of the matter seemed to be that the defenders had no heart to fight.

In four days fighting the Corps had captured 6,000 prisoners, including two Generals and an Admiral. It was ascertained that "Lord Haw Haw", the infamous broadcaster, whose voice had drawled so irritatingly over the Bremen wireless for six years, had moved his quarters to Hamburg.

Civilians went about the shattered streets trying to pretend that we were not there, while liberated Russians tied bouquets of flowers on to the tanks. On that same evening, men of the 4th/7th Dragoon Guards were sitting in their tanks in the captured town when an immaculate Jeep drove up. An equally immaculate Military Policeman got out, and unconcernedly started to nail up his sign on to an air raid shelter notice. The sign read "Club Route Up". One driver was overheard to remark: "I reckon Clubs are trumps today".

The Canadians on our left were going well, and were in the area of Emden. On our right the Guards Armoured Division had completely cut the Bremen—Hamburg Autobahn, and were nearing the Allied Prisoner of War Camp at Westertimke. Resistance in this sector was still severe, and the 15th Panzer Grenadier Division were, as usual, putting up a good fight. The Americans had already linked up with the Russians North West of Dresden, and now another junction was made at Torgau. An officer who was in Torgau sent back a laconic, but expressive report. It read simply "Much fiesta".

After the fall of Bremen the demoralised enemy was given no respite. The task of 30 Corps was to clear the peninsula between the rivers Weser and Elbe, and to capture the ports of Bremerhaven and Cuxhaven. There were not many good roads in this area, and the country was marshy. In addition the enemy was using magnetic sea mines and bombs extensively on the roads. The sea mines were particularly unpleasant, causing casualties, and blocking the roads with large craters.

On April 28th the 51st Highland Division established a bridgehead over the marshy ground to the East of Bremen, the 43rd Division, with 130 Brigade in the van used this bridgehead and advanced on Quelkhorn, where the German garrison surrendered without a fight. A troop of the 43rd Reconnaissance Regiment led the advance to the village of Bucholz, where the commander of the leading car, Sergeant Shearer, spotted a German carrying breakfast to the forward positions alongside the road. The enemy trenches were heavily mortared, but as the inmates showed no signs of surrendering, 8th Armoured Brigade tanks, and a platoon of the King's Royal Rifles passed through.

Evidently the German troops wanted to surrender, but their officer, an ardent young Nazi, fanatically refused. When the leading tank approached this officer jumped into the centre of the road with a Panzerfaust, and fired, shouting: "This is the way to fight". He was suitably dealt with, and the rest of the Germans willingly surrendered.

On the same day the Guards Armoured Division, who were pressing towards Bremervorde, again came under the command of 30 Corps. They were given the task of protecting the Northern flank of the Corps, and pushed a Brigade Group out towards Stade. The 51st Division pushed ahead on an axis parallel, and some four miles further North, to that of the 43rd Division. That evening, the 1st Battalion, The Black Watch, made contact with the Welsh Guards at Westertimke.

Meanwhile in the early morning on our right flank, elements of the Second Army had made a successful crossing of the River

Elbe, and were driving for Hamburg and Lubeck. Opposition had been less formidable than had been expected, and at least one German soldier waited patiently at the water's edge with his hands up for our assaulting troops to arrive.

In Westertimke, a Scots Guards patrol found that a British Naval Guard had already taken over the duties of the Germans at the gates of the Prisoner of War Camp. The Grenadier Guards approached the concentration camp at Sandbostel, which was defended by the enemy. After some fighting the camp was finally liberated, and its appalling contents revealed. 300 of the camp's guards were taken prisoner, and General Wuhlisc, lately Chief of Staff in Holland was also found there.

At dawn on April 29th a platoon of the 1st Motor Battalion, the Grenadier Guards, came under heavy fire in open ground West of the Sandbostel stream. The enemy was in a farm only 150 yards away, and as they had no cover, the platoon quickly suffered heavy casualties, including the platoon commander, and the platoon sergeant. Another NCO, Sergeant Clutton, returned the enemy's fire with a Bren. He took command of the platoon, organised the evacuation of the casualties, and covered their withdrawal to the river bank, which was the only cover available.

His Bren jammed owing to mud, and he lay down in a ditch full of water, still under enemy fire, and washed the gun clean. Soon afterwards it broke down again, and the Sergeant continued to give his covering fire with a rifle. For an hour and a half he covered the evacuation of the casualties, and finally withdrew himself, and although by this time he was numbed with cold and wet through, he carried with him his Bren, rifle, shovel, and all his equipment. For his gallantry in this action he was awarded the Military Medal.

The 51st Highland Division were making good progress Northwards, and on April 30th had reached the outskirts of Bremervorde, while the 43rd Division was mopping up on the East bank of the River Hamme. The village of Worpswede was occupied without resistance by men of the Somerset Light Infantry. It was an artists' colony, and was remarkable for the number of its inhabitants who volunteered to inform against each other. The village schoolmaster was said to be training the little boys for the Hitler Youth; the matron of the sanatorium, who afterwards turned out to be an aged Baroness, with 20 years nursing experience, was alleged to be a Werewolf; and an old man of some 70 summers was also said to be a Werewolf. The frightened old man turned to the crowd and cried. "Tell them I am not a Werewolf", and the delighted crowd yelled back, "Yes, you are a Werewolf".

In the early days of May disasters were falling thick and fast upon the German Reich. Berlin had fallen, yielding many thousands of prisoners, and in Northern Italy two German Armies had surrendered. In Denmark German troops were handing in their arms to the police, and in Norway some 250,000 German troops were trapped. All the roads of North West Germany were crowded with refugees, German soldiers looking for someone to whom they could surrender, and thousands of liberated slave labourers, who swarmed over the country in every direction. Tens of thousands of Allied prisoners of war also had to be dealt with, housed and fed. With Von Runstedt captured, the Fuhrer presumed dead, and whole Army Groups annihilated, final surrender was very near.

Stade surrendered on May 1st to the Guards Armoured Division, and in the South the 43rd Division made an assault crossing of the Hamme. That night the Highland Division crossed the river to the East of Bremervorde, and captured the town with its garrison of 300.

Pushing on beyond Bremervorde, a company of the 1st Battalion, the Gordon Highlanders, was ordered to capture the village of Barchel. On the way there they ran into a strong encircling counter attack. The ground was very open, and the right hand platoon was driven back, uncovering the right flank of the company. Corporal A Dale, who was commanding a section, did magnificent work in rallying his men, and kept up a very effective fire with his Bren gun.

The company commander ordered platoons to close in on some cover, but an S. P. gun had come up and was making movement difficult. In spite of the proximity of the S. P. Corporal Dale moved forward and covered the withdrawal and reorganisation of the company with more effective fire from his Bren. For his excellent example and bravery he received the Military Medal.

On May 3rd the Corps Commander was told that the Germans were negotiating for peace, but this information could not be passed down to lower formations. However, in order to save lives in the closing stages of the war in Europe, Lieutenant General Horrocks found excuses for the Divisions under his command to adopt a go-slow policy.

Hamburg had surrendered, and the Desert Rats of the 7th Armoured Division had entered the shattered city. Men of the 6th Airborne Division had reached the Baltic Coast, and linked up with the Red Army at Wismar.

On May 4th on the Corps front further advances were made and patrols of the Derbyshire Yeomanry were pushing on to Bremerhaven in the face of slight opposition. In the village of Ringstedt a German Major with a white flag approached the car troop and made the sensational announcement that our old enemies, the 15th Panzer Grenadier Division wished to surrender. Negotiations followed all day, with German and British officers discussing the arrangements for surrender, while German and British troops, armed to the teeth, walked about the village eyeing each other with deep suspicion.

Meanwhile even more important events were afoot on Luneberg Heath, for on the morning of May 3rd a delegation of senior German officers, headed by General Admiral Von Friedeburg, arrived at Field Marshal Montgomery's tactical headquarters. The German General offered surrender of the German forces in the North, but our Commander in Chief quickly made it clear that he would accept nothing else but unconditional surrender of all German land, sea, and air forces in North Western Germany, Holland and the islands. Von Friedeburg said that he had not the authority to agree to this, but when he was shown the true state of affairs on the operations map, he wept, and accepted a document incorporating, in detail, all Field Marshal Montgomery's demands. At six o'clock on Friday, May 4th, the surrender terms were signed, and at half past eight the signal was sent to our Divisions that all hostilities would cease at eight o'clock the following morning.

When the news was received there were scenes of wild rejoicing all over the Corps area. Verey lights, flares, tracer bullets, and any other form of firework which our men could lay hands on, was fired into the evening sky. Bottles of champagne, laid by in many a unit for this moment, were quickly opened, and as quickly emptied.

And so for 30 Corps came the end of the great war which had been waged so bitterly for five years and eight months. The road had been a long and weary one, starting in Alamein some three years earlier, traversing Tunis and Sicily, and picking up the trail again on the beaches of Normandy. Thence the long journey through France, Belgium, and Holland, into Germany itself.

At Bremerhaven the last of the Club Route signs had been put up, marking the end of the trail. There is a saying that the nine of diamonds is the curse of Scotland, but surely the Ace of Clubs, that solitary Club which marked the path of 30 Corps in this campaign from the beaches to Bremerhaven, signified a major curse to the Third Reich.

For whenever that simple sign appeared on the wall of a house, an old tree stump, or on a brewed up German tank, everyone knew that the boar was out hunting again.

Since Alamein, 30 Corps had had under command at one time or another a mighty array of troops. There had been no less than five armoured divisions, eleven British infantry divisions, twelve Empire divisions, an airborne division, and three American divisions.

It is not without regret that we leave Club Route, for many delightful travellers have been met on the road, and adventures along the way have been numerous. The journey has been long and the going hard, but now the men who travelled it can rest a little. In their leisure moments, perhaps, these pages will help to recall their many battles along Club Route.

*

THE BOAR AT REST. HQ 30 CORPS DISTRICT, GERMANY

On December 15th on the eve of his relinquishing command of the Corps, Lieut. General Horrocks ceremonially unveiled in a square at Nienburg, the bronze boar acquired by Rear Corps at the time of the Rhine crossing. It had been mounted on a stone plinth, made by Corps RE, the design of which had been the subject of competition, on which were engraved the battle honours of 30 Corps in both the Mediterranean and European theatres together with the emblems of First Canadian Army, Second British Army and 21 Army Group.

Symbolically it was excellent in that it effectively portrayed the end of 30 Corps war effort with the famous boar no longer rampant but at rest after his labours and his long journey along Club Route.

Lightning Source UK Ltd.
Milton Keynes UK
UKOW06f1136181114

241792UK00003B/10/P

9 781783 311033